1 MONTH OF
FREE
READING

at

www.ForgottenBooks.com

By purchasing this book you are eligible for one month membership to ForgottenBooks.com, giving you unlimited access to our entire collection of over 1,000,000 titles via our web site and mobile apps.

To claim your free month visit:

www.forgottenbooks.com/free921284

ISBN 978-0-260-00028-6
PIBN 10921284

THIRTY-FIFTH

ANNUAL REPORT

OF THE

PRESIDENT OF HARVARD COLLEGE

TO THE

OVERSEERS,

EXHIBITING

THE STATE OF THE INSTITUTION

FOR THE ACADEMICAL YEAR

1859 – 60.

CAMBRIDGE:

WELCH, BIGELOW, AND COMPANY,

PRINTERS TO THE UNIVERSITY.

1860.

THIRTY-FIFTH

ANNUAL REPORT

OF THE

PRESIDENT OF HARVARD COLLEGE

TO THE

OVERSEERS,

EXHIBITING

THE STATE OF THE INSTITUTION

FOR THE ACADEMICAL YEAR

1859–60.

CAMBRIDGE:

WELCH, BIGELOW, AND COMPANY,

PRINTERS TO THE UNIVERSITY.

1860.

REPORT.

To the Honorable and Reverend,
THE OVERSEERS OF HARVARD COLLEGE:—

THE undersigned, the President of the University, has the honor to submit the following, his First Annual Report, upon its condition during the past year.

The general state of the University has been one of great prosperity, both in the Academical Department and in the Professional Schools. In every branch of instruction the work has been ably and successfully performed. The students have faithfully devoted themselves to their studies, and have, with few exceptions, cheerfully conformed to the laws and rules which long experience has shown to be necessary for the preservation of order and discipline in such establishments. The number of students in the several departments has steadily increased, as will appear from the following table, commencing with the year 1850–51.

Year.	Undergraduates.	Professional Schools.	Total.
1850 – 51	293	303	596
1851 – 52	304	322	626
1852 – 53	319	330	649
1853 – 54	329	371	700
1854 – 55	340	365	705
1855 – 56	365	304	669
1856 – 57	382	315	697
1857 – 58	409	325	734
1858 – 59	409	321	730
1859 – 60	431	408	839
1860 – 61	443	453	896

It is a gratifying circumstance, that, at the commencement of the present term, twenty-six States were represented in the undergraduate department, — a larger number than were ever represented before, and larger by nine States than were represented ten years ago, — and the members of the Law School represented twenty-nine States. Harvard College has grown from a provincial School to a national University, comparing favorably in point of numbers and courses of instruction with the Universities of the Old World. It has still many deficiencies and wants to be supplied; and the same liberality which contributed in times past to make it what it is, may be confidently relied upon in the future for the contributions still required to make it what it should be. Large additions are needed to the general funds; an increased force is required in several departments of instruction; the salaries are insufficient for the support of the Professors' families, so that it is necessary for those who have not independent means to engage in some paying work besides their College duties. In other countries the Universities are sustained by ancient endowments, or by the resources furnished by their respective governments, from year to year. The New England Colleges must, for the most part, look to the enlightened generosity of private citizens; and it is not desirable that the highest institutions of learning should depend on legislative appropriations. The Commonwealth of Massachusetts gives generous encouragement to education, by its School Fund, by State Scholarships, and by a wisely devised system of Normal Schools. A grant has also been made in aid of the Museum of Comparative Zoölogy, which is connected with the University as a means of scientific education, though held and administered by a special board of Trustees. But the means for the increase of the Library, and the philosophical, chemical, and astronomical apparatus; for the establishment and support of the Observatory, the Scientific School, the Law School, and the Theological School; for erecting nearly all the buildings now in use as dormitories or for lectures and recitations; the endowments of all the professorships, and of all the scholarships that belong to the University, — are due to private munificence. The charges for instruction in the Academical Department are but a small fraction of the actual cost, and amount to only one half as much as those for tuition in the best private schools of this vicinity. For by far the larger part of the expenses of their instruction here, the undergraduates of Harvard University are all indebted to the charitable contributions of wise and liberal-minded citizens, who have acknowledged that wealth has its sacred duties to the moral and intellectual welfare of the present and future generations. Under these circumstances, it may reasonably be hoped that, before many years, students from every State and Territory in the Union — without a single exception or secession — will resort to our University, no difference whatever being made between the citizens of Massachusetts and the citizens of the remotest part of the country, or of foreign lands. The influence of such establishments over the young men from different and distant States must tend powerfully to remove prejudices, by bringing them into friendly relations through the humanizing effect of liberal studies pursued in common, in the impressible season of youth. Such influences are especially needed in the present disastrous condition of public affairs.

For the details of instruction in the several departments, the statements in the Appendix, together with the reports of the Examining Committees appointed by this Board, are referred to.

It is with great satisfaction that the President is enabled to report to this Board the establishment of sixteen scholarships, of two hundred and fifty dollars each, by a distinguished graduate and friend of the University. No greater benefit can be conferred upon the community than to enable young men of narrow means, but of vigorous intellect, to prepare themselves for the careers which their natural abilities and instinctive aspirations fit them for. Intellectual powers are scattered with impartial hand among the rich and the poor; and the highest good of a republican community is directly promoted by giving talent, wherever it exists, the freest scope. Young men are always to be found, in the towns and villages of our country, who sigh hopelessly for the benefits and honors of a liberal education. It is true that a person of merit and marked ability, who once succeeds in entering college, seldom fails to complete his course; but the struggle is sometimes more severe than is good for the character. Too much anxiety wears away the spirit, and self-denial may be carried too far. There are many, however, who are prevented from securing an education, by what appears to them the impossibility of doing it with slender pecuniary means. Such scholarships as those established by the late John E. Thayer, and the sixteen new scholarships just mentioned, with a few which existed before, meet the wants of just this class. Economy, sobriety, temperance, industry, are most desirable virtues to be cultivated by the young; but the effects of poverty are not of unmixed advantage. The student who is haunted by the uncertainty whether he will be able to pay any part of his term bill, is not in a favorable condition for steady application. The successful cultivation of literary and scientific studies is not promoted by the constant presence of the spectre of want. Under the rules of the founders the hope of winning a scholarship can only be cherished by those who deserve success; and when won, the income of it, while it secures the fortunate competitor from the anxieties that beset the scholar wholly destitute of means, is not sufficient to free him from the necessity of forethought, economy, and labor. He must still work for a part of the money necessary to sustain himself in college; and he must see to it that he maintains his position as a scholar of exemplary conduct in all respects, or another year may transfer the prize to worthier hands. Of all the forms by which the affluent can assist meritorious young men, this is liable to the fewest objections, and productive of the greatest benefits. A hundred such scholarships would be no more than could be disposed of among the deserving students of Harvard College to the great advantage of the country.

The President has delivered a course of Lectures during the present term, to the Freshman Class, on College Life, Duties, and Studies. His object was partly a desire to share in the work of instruction; but chiefly the hope of making suggestions to the young men who had just commenced their College course, which might warn them against the errors of opinion and conduct to which their inexperience, and some of the influences of College life, expose them. He has also delivered a course of Lectures to the Junior Class on the Language and Literature of Greece, ancient and modern.

The measures taken for the separation of the Divinity School from the College have not yet been consummated. The condition of the School, as to the means of instruction, and the earnest devotion of its members to the studies of the sacred profession which they have chosen, are highly gratifying.

The Lawrence Scientific School continues in a prosperous condition, and fulfils the purposes of its wise and liberal founder. The bequest of the late Abbott Lawrence, of fifty thousand dollars in addition to his munificent donation during his life, has been disposed of by the Commissioners under his will, and accepted by the Corporation. According to the terms agreed upon, the Professorship of Zoology and Geology has been placed on a permanent basis. Mr. Henry James Clarke, who has long been associated with Professor Agassiz as a student and private assistant, and who has shown a remarkable genius for original investigation in Natural History, has been appointed Assistant Professor of Zoölogy; but at present no salary is attached to the office.

It is hoped that the means may be found to secure him permanently in that department.

The Law School has not only maintained, but surpassed, its former prosperity. As has been already mentioned, the students have been drawn from twenty-nine States. They have pursued their studies with exemplary diligence, and, while the discords of the country have been increasing, they have lived in uninterrupted harmony. The Law Library needs to be enlarged; and it is hoped that a Professorship of Roman Law may in time be added to its means of instruction.

The work of the Observatory has gone forward as usual. For the details, the Board is referred to the report of the Director made to their Committee. A year ago the Director represented to the Committee the importance of publishing the materials which had been collected for a history of the phenomena of the great comet of 1858, and exhibited to them the drawings which had been prepared to accompany it. The cost of the publication was estimated at five thousand dollars. Two gentlemen, members of the Observatory Committee, have generously undertaken to furnish the means of publishing the text with the engravings, and the work has been in progress since last April. It will probably be completed within the time originally contemplated, namely, two years from its commencement.

Among the interesting events of the present term,

two may be specially mentioned. ·On the 19th of October, the Prince of Wales, with his distinguished suite, visited the University. He was cordially welcomed by the undergraduates as an undergraduate. He was received in Gore Hall by the academical bodies, and visited in succession all the departments of the University, the Professors giving brief explanations of the resources and arrangements of their several departments. The Prince manifested the intelligent interest of an educated young man, in the institution; and the day was in all respects highly interesting to the members of the University.

The other event alluded to was the dedication of the Museum of Comparative Zoölogy, which took place on the 13th of November. A large number of the friends of the establishment assembled at the Museum, and proceeded thence to the church, which had been fitted up as usual for Commencement. The church was filled by an assemblage of cultivated people, who listened with interest to the services of the occasion. The Museum was opened immediately after for the public, and the following week Professor Agassiz commenced the course of lectures to which, according to the law, the teachers in the public schools were to be admitted. Two lectures a week were delivered at such times as suited the convenience of the teachers, until the end of the term. The lecture-room has been constantly crowded. This wise provision on the part of the Commonwealth will result in great benefits to the public instruction of the schools, and will thus in a few years more than repay the munificent endowment which the State has granted to the Museum.

The building thus far completed is only a part of a comprehensive plan; but it enjoys the advantage of having been constructed after long and careful study of the details in reference to its objects and use, by the most distinguished architectural skill in concert with the scientific views of Professor Agassiz. The collection has been arranged, so far as the time and means have allowed, according to the principles of classification established by the last results of scientific investigation; so that what has been once done will never need to be undone; and the facilities afforded for study and practical use are all that can be desired. But the present building is sufficient for a part only of the collections, which are accumulating daily from every quarter of the world. The liberality of the public must be looked to for the additional means necessary to make it a museum of the first class. If such means are furnished, it may become, within the lifetime of the present generation, equal in comprehensiveness to any in the world, as it will undoubtedly be superior in arrangement to the most celebrated now existing. We may hope that its establishment will not only be a great and lasting benefit to the common-school system of Massachusetts, but that it will be the means, in all future time, of drawing hither noble young men, fired with the love of nature, who shall bear hence the lights of science to illuminate the world. Its benefits are already felt at home, and it has excited the admiration of the wisest men from abroad. If its future destiny corresponds to the good omens of present success, we may not unreasonably look to it as one of the great landmarks of science for mankind.

The report of the Librarian presents a gratifying view of the prosperity of that most important department of the University. Mr. William Gray's benefaction has already added materially to the utility and the use of the Library. Since July, 1859, ten thousand dollars have been received from him. The money has been distributed by a committee among the several departments, the Professors in which have been called upon to furnish lists of books. Faithful and competent purchasing agents have been employed in Europe. The efficiency of every department has been greatly increased. Every scholar who has occasion to consult the Library has reason for gratitude to this enlightened and generous benefactor. The donation of the Hon. Stephen Salisbury, creating a fund of five thousand dollars for the purchase of Greek and Latin literature, is yearly adding important works to that department of the Library. It has been expended in accordance with his instructions, contained in a letter to President

Walker, of November 23, 1858, and directing that it should be "invested safely and productively, and maintained as a separate fund, of which the annual income shall be expended in the purchase of books in the Greek and Latin languages, and in books in other languages illustrating the Greek and Latin." The library of the late Clarke Gayton Pickman, consisting of more than three thousand well-chosen volumes of standard works in English literature, left by will to the University, was promptly and courteously delivered by his executor, J. A. Loring, Esq. It is a very valuable collection. Many of the books are elegantly bound. Some of the most important works were not in the Library before ; particular editions of others were wanting; others are duplicates, but in almost every case they are books of which it is desirable to have several copies, and which will be constantly useful in a working library. All who habitually use the Library will cherish the memory of the generous son of Harvard, who, in disposing of his worldly goods, remembered his Alma Mater in so filial a manner. Many volumes have been received as gifts from authors and publishers, all of which have been enumerated in the elaborate and minute report of the Librarian.

Professor Cooke was absent by leave a few months last summer in Europe. Before embarking he received by the contributions of friends the sum of eight hundred dollars, to which was added an unexpended balance, amounting to a thousand dollars, of a fund formerly raised by subscription for the Mineralogical Cabinet. Of this sum the Professor expended about fourteen hundred dollars for minerals, and the remainder for apparatus, in order to complete, so far as possible, the Mineralogical Cabinet. The collection, which before represented about one half of the mineralogical species, now contains representatives of nearly all, and is sufficient for the purposes of instruction. Though not so rich in unique specimens as several other Cabinets in the country, in scientific value and adequacy to the wants of the teacher it is equal to any. Professor Cooke also purchased the apparatus for illustrating the remarkable discoveries recently made by Plucher and Bunsen on the nature of light emanating from different chemical elements and its use in chemical analysis, as well as the apparatus invented by Becquerel for illustrating the phenomena of phosphorescence.

Professor Huntington having resigned his place, after five years of earnest and devoted service, his resignation was accepted at the close of the year, and a special arrangement was made with him by the President to perform or provide for the duties of the office until the end of the following term. The Rev. A. P. Peabody, who was in the mean time appointed to the Plummer Professorship, commenced his duties at the beginning of the present term. His labors have been highly acceptable, both as a teacher and as the University Preacher.

The undersigned, having resigned the Eliot Professorship of Greek Literature, continued to perform the duties of the office to the end of the Academic year, in order to complete a course of instruction which, not anticipating any change, he had laid down for the whole year. Mr. William W. Goodwin, who had shown high scholarship and ability as Tutor in the department, was elected Eliot Professor; and Mr. Evangelinus A. Sophocles, the Assistant Professor of Greek, was elected to a newly established Professorship, entitled the University Professorship of Ancient, Patristic (including the Byzantine), and Modern Greek. Both these gentlemen entered upon their respective offices at the commencement of the present term. This arrangement of the Greek Department is highly satisfactory. It was thought important to provide the means of instruction in the Ecclesiastical Greek, should any desire it, in reference to their future theological studies. The Modern Greek has for many years constituted a part of the regular course, having been introduced by the undersigned in conformity to a suggestion of the Founder of the Professorship. Its importance is now much greater than it was at the time when Mr. Eliot, with wise forecast, inserted the provision alluded to in the articles of the Professorship. The language and literature of the independent kingdom of Greece are rapidly rising to a position which will command the respect of the literary world. The Modern Greek is the medium of intercourse throughout the Levant; and it is a great convenience to travellers in those countries, the number of whom yearly increases, to understand that language.

The President cannot leave this topic without expressing his gratitude to the successive Committees of Examination, appointed by the Overseers, during the long period in which he has held the Greek Professorship. A large proportion of the members have been gentlemen having a special taste for Greek Literature, and all of them have been classical scholars. They have shown remarkable punctuality in attending to the duties assigned them, great interest in the department, and a candid appreciation of every effort made to raise the standard of Greek study. Their reports have been valuable to the cause of classical education. Some of them have attracted the attention and received the applause of European scholars; and those on the study of Modern Greek have been translated into that language, and published in the literary journals of Athens. The President retired from the Greek Department with a regret which time has not yet begun to lessen; and the pleasant relations so long maintained between him and the Greek Examining Committees will always be remembered.

Professor Peirce, after an uninterrupted service of twenty-seven years, received leave of absence last summer for the purpose of travel in Europe, on account of impaired health; Professor Sophocles was absent for part of the Summer term to visit his country and family after a long separation; and Mr. Schmitt, the German teacher, was obliged to be absent a few weeks at the close of the Summer and the beginning of the Autumn term. Mr. Jennison, the Tutor in Elocution, at the commencement of the present term received leave of absence for six months, on account of impaired health; and early in December Professor Eustis, of the Scientific School, received leave of absence for six months, also on account of impaired health. In all these cases, satisfactory arrangements have been made for the instruction, without additional expense to the College.

Besides the appointments already mentioned, it has been found necessary to increase the force in the Library, and the services of Mr. Charles Ammi Cutter have been secured in Mr. Abbot's department; Mr. James Jennison has been appointed Tutor in Elocution; Mr. Andrew Tucker Bates, Tutor in Latin and History.

Mr. Thies, the Curator of the Gray Collection of Engravings, is making progress in the preparation of a complete and thorough descriptive catalogue. Two cabinets have been added for the great works of Audubon and Rossellini. Several valuable donations have been received from Mr. Charles Eliot Norton, of works illustrating the early period of Tuscan art. It is stated by Mr. Thies that this is the best private collection in the world for engravings of the works of Rafael. It is earnestly desired that the means of studying the arts, at least so far as that study bears upon education, may in time be secured to the College. It is now possible, at a comparatively small expense, to make a collection of plaster copies of the best works in sculpture, ancient and modern. Instruction in the classics may be made more interesting and useful by the illustration to be afforded by copies of the Elgin and Egina Marbles, and the other well-known specimens of Greek art, preserved in the European galleries. Photographs of works in every department of art serve an excellent purpose in lectures upon these subjects, and in general teaching; and as they can be easily and cheaply procured, there is no reason why this kind of illustration should not be extensively used.

Mr. George Washington Wales has presented to the Library a marble bust of his brother, the late Dr. Wales, to whom the College is indebted for the beautiful Wales Library; a marble bust of Christopher Gore, executed by Miss Lander, has been given by friends of the College; and a new bust of the late Dr. Kirkland has been substituted in the Library by the artist, Mr. T. A. Carew, for the smaller one made some years before. The class graduated at the last Commencement have presented a portrait of President Walker, painted for this purpose by the distinguished artist, Mr. William Hunt. It has been placed in the gallery of Harvard Hall.

The want of a building for the annual meetings of the Graduates, and for other public purposes, is more strongly felt than ever. At the last Commencement, it was found necessary to return to the former rule, which restricted admission to the Commencement Dinner to Masters of Arts, the academic bodies, and invited guests; excluding the three most recent classes. Notwithstanding this restriction, every place was occupied. For several years previously the crowd had been so great, and the rush to obtain seats so annoying, that the older graduates were reluctant to expose themselves to the confusion, and had begun to absent themselves from the Commencement festival. To withdraw a privilege once granted, no matter how urgent the reasons for taking the step, always creates dissatisfaction; and it was not surprising that this proceeding of the University gave some offence. But it was right and necessary. With a hall large enough to receive the whole body of graduates, it would have been more agreeable to assemble them all. In the actual circumstances of the case, the choice lay between admitting the oldest classes, who have paid for the dinner by charges on their term bills, and the

younger, who have not paid anything, — the charge
in question having been discontinued several years
ago. A hall is greatly needed for the services of
Commencement Day. The church, which the College have the right to occupy on their public days,
was never a very suitable building for such exercises; at present it is not only insufficient in size,
but is rapidly falling into decay, and cannot be ex-
pected to be even safe many years longer.

Mr. John C. Gray, as was mentioned in former
reports, established two mathematical prizes for the
year 1860, and again for 1861, of two hundred and
fifty dollars each. The prizes for 1860 were awarded,
after a severe examination by a special committee,
towards the close of the Summer term. The same
liberal-minded gentleman has offered the same sum
for two prizes in 1862. It would be very desirable to multiply such inducements to special studies,
by establishing prizes in the departments of Classics,
Physical Science, and Philosophy.

Physical exercise has, of late years, received a
large share of public attention, in connection with
sedentary pursuits. This is right; and the public attention has been properly awakened to the importance
of the subject. But no man ever killed himself by
hard study alone. The exercise of the intellectual
faculties is not only pleasurable, but healthy. The
brain is a physical organ; and the vigorous use of
it in its appropriate function, as an instrument of

the mind, conduces to bodily health. The statistics of life prove conclusively that diligent study tends to length of days. Many evils have resulted to sedentary men, not from study, but from the neglect of exercise ; they have injured their health, and perhaps shortened their lives, by forgetting the laws on which the preservation of health and life depends; but these evils are now in a fair way of being remedied in our schools and colleges. The subject requires prudent management, or the introduction of the systems of exercise now recommended will do as much harm as good. There is a tendency to exaggeration and extravagance. The language of some of the recent discussions seems to imply that muscular development is identical with moral, intellectual, and religious progress. It seems to be thought the panacea for all the evils under which humanity labors. Extraordinary feats of strength are heralded by the telegraph as events on which the welfare of society depends. We have lately seen two great nations in a state of intense excitement, while awaiting the result of a brutal conflict between two prize-fighters, whose chief merit was that of having beaten each other out of all resemblance to human beings. More surprising still, the phrase " muscular Christianity " has become a current commonplace in the literature of the day, — as if thews, sinews, and muscles, and not the Sermon on the Mount, contained the essential points of the Christian religion. These are the excesses to which ill-balanced judgments are constantly running. Bodily strength is a good thing, but it is not the best thing. It is a help to the intellect, but it is not identical with intellect. It facilitates the vigorous performance of the duties of life, without being the essence of morality and religion. But an abnormal condition of physical strength is neither good in itself, nor likely to prolong life. Many of those who have rendered the noblest services to humanity, who have achieved the most illustrious triumphs in art, literature, science, and philanthropy, have been men of delicate constitutions and feeble health. The amount of labor performed in the most exalted tasks has never borne any proportion to the muscular development. But it is not intended to say that physical vigor, and a healthy activity of all the forces of the body, are not proper objects of desire, and ought not to command the serious attention of those who have charge of the education of the young. Their importance was fully recognized by that nation to whom we owe the largest intellectual debt. But, on both moral and physical grounds, we must guard against extremes. "Nothing to excess," was an ancient maxim of universal application. The wise men of antiquity applied it to this very subject, and they drew the line firmly between proper gymnastic exercise, for the cultivation of vigor and beauty, as

curative processes and gentlemanlike accomplish-
ments, as a part of the education of the boy and
the daily recreation of the man, on the one hand,
and the training of the athletes on the other.
The former they regarded as essential to a sound
mind in a sound body; the latter, as mischievous
and immoral. And, indeed, it must be evident
that, to occupy the mind and time with a system
of physical exercises, for the purpose of enlarg-
ing to the utmost possible extent the strength and
volume of the muscles, is inconsistent with the
thorough training of the intellectual and moral nature. It is the training of a pugilist and a prize-
fighter, and not the liberal culture of a scholar and
gentleman. It is lavishing upon the lower and
mortal part of our being the priceless gift of time
and thought which are due only to the higher and
immortal.

Recognizing fully the importance of physical
health, the authorities of the University have encouraged every form of exercise fitted to conduce
to that end. The Gymnasium, founded by an un-
known benefactor, has been regarded with unanimous
favor. Tutors and professors, no less than students,
have availed themselves of the opportunity of healthy
exercise it affords. A judicious system of gymnas-
tics is, for various reasons, deserving of the attention
of studious men. It is so flexible that it can be
adapted to any kind of constitution, and to every

part of every constitution. It can be employed efficaciously in restoring lost strength, or in preserving and increasing strength that has been acquired. Its action on the vital organs is especially beneficial. Another great recommendation of it is the economy of time. Twenty minutes of vigorous gymnastic practice, with moderate exercise in the open air, every day, is better for the student than many hours of mere walking. During the forming period of the physical constitution, it is especially useful in correcting natural defects, and promoting an equal and well-balanced growth of all the parts of the body. When this period is passed, the health so acquired may be easily preserved by simple means, and with no loss of time, by making some of the common exercises a part of the morning toilet, with the bath, warm or cold. Unless some such continuation of the practice is adopted, the good effects of gymnastic training cannot be made permanent. The Gymnasium in Cambridge has now been in operation a year and a half. The number of persons availing themselves of it has been constantly between four and five hundred. The College has been fortunate in securing the services of a gymnastic teacher, who is not only master of his profession, but a man of excellent judgment. Under his supervision not a single accident has happened to any member of the classes; and only a few to persons using the apparatus by themselves.

Of late years the exercise of boating has been introduced to a considerable extent. This is doubtless excellent in the main; but there are dangers to be guarded against. Of itself, rowing conduces to vigor; and the temperance and self-denial necessary to thorough training are an admirable discipline. But it may be questioned whether the violent strain upon youthful constitutions, incident to the desire for victory in the race, is not too full of danger to be encouraged. It is feared that some have been permanently injured by excessive efforts; and perhaps lives have been shortened. Another objection to boating is its expense; for this reason, no student is permitted to become a member of a boat-club without the express sanction of his parent or guardian, in writing. In its very nature it is less under control than the gymnastic system; and the temptations to young and inexperienced men, ignorant of physiological laws, and full of animal spirits and eager emulation, are very serious. These things are mentioned, not with any purpose of interfering with healthful and pleasurable exercises, but with the hope of making useful suggestions, and indicating precautions which are thought necessary to secure the greatest possible amount of benefit with the least possible harm, from the revival of manly sports.

It is much to be desired that, in connection with this subject, a Professorship of Hygiene should be established. The services of a skilful and experienced physician, who shall act as the friend and adviser of the students, are greatly needed. Brought together from their homes, at a critical age, without the oversight of parents or family physicians, many, no doubt, fall into habits injurious to health, without being conscious of the dangers they are incurring; many are careless of precautions which are forced upon them at home; some are drawn into temptations with regard to eating, drinking, and smoking, which they need to be warned against. The College rules of order in some measure help to protect the students from these dangers; but a good physician in the department of hygiene, who, as professor, should give them instruction, by lectures or otherwise, at the commencement of the College course, and to whom they might resort in all cases of illness, whose advice they should have the right to ask confidentially on all matters relating to health, and who should exercise a controlling direction whenever a student appeared to suffer from bad habits, ignorance, or neglect, would be the best possible safeguard. The importance of such a professorship can hardly be exaggerated. The Trustees of Amherst College have already supplied this urgent want by the appointment of a competent professor. They have set a good example, which it would be well to follow, and it is earnestly hoped that the friends of Harvard will see to it that the students, especially the undergraduates, enjoy the like security.

The advantages of a college training are so great and permanent, that no one can hesitate a moment in admitting that they outweigh its dangers and defects. An unhappy result is the rare exception; the rule that good, useful, and able men are formed under its discipline, is almost uniform. Still every human system has its evils and imperfections. It is a good thing for a young man to be thrown upon his own resources, to be removed from the partialities and flatteries of home, to learn self-knowledge by measuring himself with others who will not spare him the necessity of doing his best. Such is the situation of the student at college. But it is an evil for a young man to feel that he belongs to a community, the peculiar organization of which gives such force to wayward opinions, that acts not tolerated elsewhere in civilized society are endured, and their authors protected. To some extent this is the case with all educational institutions where young persons are brought together in close companionship; but it is the duty of those who have them in charge to prevent the evil consequences of a mischievous corporate sentiment by correcting the sentiment itself so far as they possibly can.

The English practice of making drudges out of the new-comers, under the name of fagging, and the custom which has grown up in American colleges of annoying the newly entered class by a process called hazing, are utterly reprehensible; and nothing but a false and unnatural sentiment among the members of the English schools and the students of American colleges would have yielded a moment's toleration to such barbarisms. The evil in this country increases with the growth of colleges, and has become so serious that the attention of the public has been anxiously called to it. Parents have serious doubts about sending their sons to college the first year; those who overcome their fears are in a state of painful apprehension until the year is past. There is perhaps some exaggeration in the common description of these abuses; but, making all deductions on this account, there is no question that serious outrages on the persons, property, and domiciles of the younger members have been perpetrated for many years past in our colleges. It is quite certain that most of these acts have originated in a reckless love of fun, and not in a criminal purpose deliberately formed. But students are not boys: they are of a responsible age; and in any other society they would not dare to violate the rights of the youngest person; they could not do these things without arousing a storm of public indignation, and exposing themselves to the animadversion of the law. Any society which fails to protect *all* its members, however feeble or young, in their persons and property, so far fails to accomplish the objects of a civilized community. A practical joke is bad enough; it is always vulgar and witless. If this were all, the matter might be left to correct itself; but midnight assaults upon defenceless persons, or upon their rooms, the breaking of windows and destruction of furniture, are something more, — they are cowardly and criminal. The possibility of a single such act in a society of scholars — of persons accustomed to the amenities of polished society, and governed by the spirit of gentlemen in their other relations — is surprising.*

It is the natural dictate of generosity to protect the young, and to receive the stranger with hospitality. The practice in question reverses this, and encourages acts which are ungenerous, inhospitable, and tyrannical. As the number of students increases, the evils and dangers become greater. There is reason to believe that in some cases the health of

---

* A distinguished graduate of Harvard, the Rev. Dr. Osgood of New York, has lately published an admirable little volume, entitled "Student Life: Letters and Recollections for a Young Friend." It ought to be placed in the hands of every youth intending to enter College. The following passage has an important bearing upon this subject : —

"The injustice that is the offspring of false honor shows itself in college in various ways, sometimes in annoying fellow-students, sometimes in assaulting or plundering the townspeople, and sometimes by conspiring against the college government. Sometimes, indeed, a certain passion for fun is more prominent than any depraved spirit of mischief; yet such fun, when persistently pursued, ends in habitual mischief, and has left a mark upon many a youth's fortune and disposition that years cannot obliterate. 'In every class there is more or less disposition to oppress the more sensitive of its own members, whilst there is a standing custom of annoying to the utmost all novices in the lower classes. I have no objection to giving the greenhorns a little good-natured initiation, but when it comes to per-the victims has been seriously broken. And there is another danger. Every man, young or old, has a right to defend his person from lawless assaults, and the blame and peril, whatever means he may resort to, belong to the assailant. It would be a great misfortune should blood be shed in resisting such outrages; but if they are allowed to go on, this result will be inevitable. Youths of a courageous temper and a quick sense of honor will not submit to personal degradation. They will arm themselves with deadly weapons, and will use them in self-defence. The Faculty of Harvard College have always regarded these reckless acts as grave offences, and have punished their authors, when detected, with summary dismission.

The annual game of football had degenerated into a fight between the Classes, in which serious injuries were inflicted. Information was given to

sonal insults, injury to property, falsehood, and theft, the joke goes too far; and I have known outrages to be committed by students upon their fellows, especially of the younger classes, that no sophistry could call by any other name than ruffianly and dastardly, as mean as they were insolent, because so sure of doing harm with impunity." — pp. 68, 69.

The offences enumerated in the following sentences have nearly become obsolete. It is well that their true character should be pointed out. The remark in the last sentence is as true as it is important.

" As to wrongs to persons outside the college walls, such as are done in street-fights, robbery of orchards and hen-roosts, it is important to remember that the Homeric age has passed away, that piracy is no longer heroism, and to knock down a policeman or to plunder farms is felony. The sooner students understand that they are bound by the law of the land, the better for their morals and their mirth, and the sooner they will be moved to let their neighbor's goods alone, and to seek sport in more free and congenial fields." — pp. 69, 70.

the President by parents and teachers, that it was a growing custom of scholars preparing to enter college to take lessons in sparring and boxing, by way of qualification for the football match at the opening of the term. And it was known to him, from the testimony of persons who had witnessed, and of others who had taken part in the contest, that it was no longer a manly trial of skill and strength, but a struggle of brute force, — not only utterly unfit for the members of a university, but dangerous to life and limb.

For these reasons, the Faculty thought themselves called upon imperatively, the past year, to put a stop to the football meeting and to "hazing," and they passed a vote directing the President to take the necessary measures. He accordingly sent a circular to the parents of those to whom the votes referred, informing them of the course the Faculty had adopted, and requesting them to use their influence in persuading their sons voluntarily to discontinue these abuses; and before the end of the term he made a personal appeal to the Class. At the commencement of the following term he addressed them again, urging them as scholars, Christians, and gentlemen not to continue practices so unsuitable to the place, and so severely condemned by a just public opinion. Many of the parents responded, entirely approving the determination which the Faculty had taken on both the matters included in their votes. Indeed, there was not, so far as known, a single dissenting opinion among the parents of the students, or the public generally. The President is satisfied that more than nine tenths of the students themselves desired that such unscholarly and unlawful usages should cease. It was believed that all would yield a ready compliance with requirements so necessary and reasonable. The annual meeting of the Classes for the football match was abandoned; and it was hoped that the other and still more objectionable practice would be discontinued with equal readiness. The President regrets to say that this hope was not entirely realized, and the Faculty found themselves compelled, in the course of the present term, to carry their resolve into effect by several acts of discipline. It is earnestly hoped that these may be the last punishments for such offences. The President has no hesitation in saying, that, if the present organization of the College is insufficient for the protection of its members from such wanton outrages, then the organization should be changed; for the security of person, property, and domicile of every member of college is a condition which must be insisted on at any cost. If college laws are inadequate to establish this principle, then it will be the duty of the academical authorities to resort to other measures. If the peculiar forms and influences of college life should be found to interfere with the just and equal rights of all the members, then the forms of college life should be modified. If the system of classes, and the assembling of students in college buildings, separated in some measure from the common influences of society, create inevitably a public sentiment which defies and resists authority and perpetuates barbarous abuses, then college classes should be broken up, the buildings used for other purposes, and the entire system reconstructed, so that each young man shall be, like young men in other conditions of life, directly and individually responsible for his acts.

Such an alternative, however, is not likely to be presented. It cannot be doubted that a very large majority of the young men will, in good time, not only acquiesce in, but support a principle right in itself and essential to their highest interests.

But it is very clear, that, with the increasing number of students, the responsibility of each and all to the laws of the land — a principle which has always been embodied in the laws of the College — must be the rule, and not the exception, whenever serious infractions of the law are committed. The College Faculty is not a body that can well investigate such offences. Its members have no power to place witnesses on the stand, or to administer an oath; and if they had, they cannot inflict punishment upon conviction of the offender. The highest penalty they can impose is expulsion from College. The division of the students into classes has much to recommend it. Among classmates a strong and peculiar friendship, formed by equality of age, similarity of pursuits, and intimate association for four years of the plastic period of youth, springs up, and lasts through the longest life. In such an organization, however, the members of a class can never be brought to bear witness against each other, or against fellow-students of other classes, in examinations before the College Faculty; and they ought not to be required to do this, in ordinary cases of college discipline. As students, their relation to each other is not analogous to that of citizen to citizen ; and the College government is not a political or judicial body of their own creating. Recognizing these truths, the Faculty of Harvard College never require a student to testify before them against his fellows.

But there is another side to the picture. The close union between classmates sometimes gives a pernicious power to the evil-disposed, and establishes maxims of conduct at variance with the principles elsewhere universally admitted. It affords a ready means of banding together in opposition to the discipline absolutely necessary for the accomplishment of the very purposes for which they came to the University. The lawless and wilful spirit thus generated sometimes draws the best disposed and most orderly in their general conduct, by the contagious excitement of sympathy, into acts which they deplore when the frenzy has run its course. It is thought this evil may be checked, and the consequences of these paroxysms of insubordination avoided, if it is understood once for all that serious violations of the law shall be dealt with by the appropriate tribunals. The temporary and abnormal influences of college association cease in the presence of public justice. The witness must take the stand, whether student or apprentice, young or old, rich or poor, and is compelled to aid, to the extent of his knowledge, in the discovery of the truth. Deeds of violence and personal outrage ought to be put down by the force of a sound public opinion among the students themselves; but this will never be effected so long as the theory prevails that the College premises are inaccessible to the operation of the laws of the land, — so long as the perpetrators of such deeds can rely upon the protection of their fellow-students, and are allowed to suppose, however erroneously, that they are only amenable to a college faculty, who have, as they are well aware, no adequate power.

The principle of responsibility to the laws has always been recognized here; but when the number of students was small, the discipline of the College and the authority of the Faculty were sufficient, except in cases that occurred at long intervals. In this age our American Colleges are rapidly becoming great Universities; student life is assuming larger proportions, and acquiring a more commanding position; it is growing every year more important that principles of justice which regulate all civilized society should be incorporated in the system of academical government; that boyish mischief and headstrong passion, and the tyranny of senseless customs, should be restrained, and manly obedience to lawful authority, and respect for each other's personal rights as gentlemen and scholars, become the universal rule. The parietal and domestic government, which formerly served the purpose of maintaining order sufficiently well, cannot much longer be regarded as a fit substitute for the legal responsibilities to which all other citizens are at all times and under all circumstances subjected.

This subject has been dwelt upon somewhat at length because at this moment there is no question of more vital importance to the continued prosperity of the College.

It must not be inferred that the disorderly acts referred to have extended to any considerable number of the students, or that they have been more common than usual during the period embraced in this report. On the contrary, it is believed that fewer flagrant instances have occurred than in preceding years. But the subject is now brought to the attention of the Board, because special efforts have been made to put an end to these particular offences ; and because a period has arrived in the progress of the University when, according to the best judgment of the undersigned, its future welfare and good name require that an end be put to them forever, let the immediate consequences be what they may. The moral and religious condition of the society, — the temperance, order, and industry which have been its general characteristics, — the growing sense of the sacred and immutable obligations of truth, of which striking proofs have been given within the past year, — inspire the hope that whatever is amiss in college opinion and practice upon the points in question will be corrected by the good sense and right feeling of the students, in accordance with the progress of Christian civilization and an enlightened public opinion.

All of which is respectfully submitted.

C. C. FELTON, *President.*

CAMBRIDGE, December 31, 1860.

APPENDIX.

I.

Summary Statement of the Course of Instruction pursued in the several Departments of the University during the Academical Year 1859–60.

I. ACADEMICAL DEPARTMENT.

1. Religious Instruction.

Instruction in " Christian Morals," and in the " Christian Evidences," has been regularly given by Frederic D. Huntington, D. D., Preacher to the University and Plummer Professor of Christian Morals. During the First Term of the year he heard recitations from the Freshman Class, twice a week, in Whately's Lessons on Christian Morals and Christian Evidences, a text-book that has been substituted for Whewell and Paley.

Lectures on the Special Duties and Exposures of a College Life have been delivered by this Professor to the same Class.

The service of Daily Prayers has been attended by him, in the Chapel. He has also been responsible for the supply of the Chapel Pulpit on Sundays.

Other religious exercises, at which the attendance is voluntary, have been conducted by the same officer.

Professor Huntington having resigned his place at the close of the First Term, the President was authorized to make a special arrangement with him to perform the customary duties of the office, or to provide for them, until the end of the Academic year.

At present, two hundred and thirteen students have leave of absence from Cambridge to pass Sunday at home; one hundred and forty-seven attend worship in the College Chapel; and eighty-three attend other churches in Cambridge.

2. PHILOSOPHY.

The means of instruction in this Department are lectures, recitations, familiarly illustrated at the time by the Professor, and written forensic exercises.

The Department was under the charge of Francis Bowen, A. M., Alford Professor. During the first Academic Term, the Senior Class recited four times a week in Reid's Essays on the Intellectual Powers and Bowen's Ethics and Metaphysics. During the Second Term, the same Class recited six times a week in Bowen's Political Economy and Hamilton's Metaphysics. The Class recited in three Divisions, on the first four days of the week, so that the recitation of each day occupied three hours.

Forensics were read, throughout the year, every Tuesday forenoon, by the Seniors, half of the Class attending each week.

All the instruction in this Department is now given to the Senior Class.

3. RHETORIC AND ORATORY.

This Department is under the superintendence of Francis J. Child, Boylston Professor of Rhetoric and Oratory, assisted in the teaching of Elocution by James Jennison, A.M.

Instruction in this Department is given to the three upper Classes, by exercises in Reading, Speaking, and English Composition, and by recitations in Grammar and Rhetoric.*

The Sophomores, during the First Term of the current year, studied Vernon's Anglo-Saxon Guide.

One fourth of the Class wrote Themes, and attended a critical exercise upon them, every week throughout the year.

To the Juniors instruction was given by recitations, twice a week, during the Second Term, from Whately's Rhetoric.

They write Themes, and attend a critical exercise upon them, once every two weeks, through the year.

They also declaim, by sections of nine, every week, before the Class and the instructors.

---

* Logic, which has of late years formed part of the instruction in this Department, is now transferred to the Department of Philosophy.

The inspection of performances for Commencement and other Public Exhibitions is committed to this Department.

The foregoing statement relates to the duties of the Professor.

In addition to the exercises in Declamation already mentioned, there is a separate course of instruction in Elocution, which is wholly under the care of the Instructor in Elocution.

Nine Juniors attended him every week in an exercise preparatory to the weekly Declamation of the Class.

The Sophomores and Freshmen attended him once every week, during the year.

He superintended the rehearsals of performances for the Public Exhibitions of the year; the final rehearsal for each of which is regularly attended by the Professor.

Leave of absence having been granted to Professor Child, his place, during a part of the First Term, was supplied by Mr. Jennison.

4. HISTORY.

Instruction was given in this Department to the Senior Class, during the last academical year, by the Professor of History. The books used were Guizot's Lectures on the History of Civilization in France and in Europe, Hallam's Constitutional History, with the Student's Hume, and Sheppard's Constitutional Text-Book. The Class recited four times a week during the year, and were examined by written questions and orally at the end of the Second Term. A course of Lectures was also read to the Class at the close of the year. The Freshman Class recited twice a week during the Second Term to Mr. Jennison, the Tutor in History, in Liddell's History of Rome, and were examined by written questions and orally at the end of that Term.

5. LATIN.

During the past year this Department was under the superintendence of George M. Lane, University Professor of Latin, assisted by Ephraim W. Gurney, Edwin H. Abbot, and Solomon Lincoln, Tutors. The instruction of the Senior and Junior Classes was conducted by Professor Lane, that of the Sophomore Class by Mr. Gurney, and that of the Freshman Class by Mr. Abbot and Mr. Lincoln.

Instruction was given to the Freshman Class in Lincoln's Selections from Livy, the Odes of Horace, Roman Antiquities, and in writing Latin, once a month.

To the Sophomore Class, in the Satires of Horace, and Cicero's Oration for Sestius, and in writing Latin, once a month.

To the Junior Class, in the Eunuchus of Terence and a part of the Annals of Tacitus, and in writing Latin prose and verse.

To the Seniors, in Tibullus, and in writing Latin prose.

In the three lower Classes the Latin was a required study ; with the Seniors it was elective.

---

6. Greek.

The Greek Department was under the care of Cornelius Conway Felton, LL.D., Eliot Professor of Greek Literature, and Evangelinus A. Sophocles, A. M., Assistant Professor of Greek, William W. Goodwin, P.D., and Solomon Lincoln, A.B., Tutors.

The Freshmen were instructed by Mr. Sophocles and Mr. Lincoln. They were divided into four alphabetical Sections. The text-books during the First Term were Homer's Odyssey and the Panegyricus of Isocrates ; during the Second Term, the Oration of Lycurgus against Leocrates. There were five recitations a week during each Term, besides an exercise every fortnight in Greek Prose Composition.

The Sophomores were instructed by Mr. Goodwin. They were divided into four alphabetical Sections, each Section reciting three times a week. They read the Olynthiacs and Philippics during the First Term, and parts of the Orations against Aristocrates and against Timocrates during the Second Term.

The Juniors and Seniors were instructed by the Professor.

The Seniors and Juniors attended three exercises each week. The Professor also delivered a course of public Lectures to the Junior Class, on Greek Literature, one Lecture being delivered each week during the First Term.

The Juniors recited in three alphabetical Sections. In the First Term, they read the Ajax of Sophocles, and the Clouds of Aristophanes ; in the Second Term, the Clouds of Aristophanes, and parts of the Iliad.

A Section of eighteen Seniors selected the Greek as an elective study. They read Demosthenes against the Law of Leptines, against Meidias, and against Androtion, in the First Term ; and the Agamemnon of Æschylus in the Second Term.

7. HEBREW.

This Department was under the superintendence of the Rev. George R. Noyes, D.D., Hancock Professor of Hebrew and other Oriental Languages; being conducted by recitations and oral instruction, given to members of the Senior Class three times each week, during the year, if desired. Attendance on this branch is optional. During the past year five members of the Senior Class have pursued the study of Hebrew, and have made very satisfactory progress.

8. MODERN LANGUAGES.

This Department was under the superintendence of James R. Lowell, A.M., Smith Professor of the French and Spanish Languages, and Professor of the Belles-Lettres. There were in the Department two Instructors : Charles Miel, A. M., Instructor in French, and George Adam Schmitt, Instructor in German.*

The principles which regulate the Department are, — 1. All the Modern Languages are optional. 2. A student commencing the study of any language is not permitted to leave it before the close of the year without a vote of the Faculty. 3. The students are formed into Sections, and are carried forward according to their proficiency, without reference to Classes. 4. The days of instruction are Mondays, Wednesdays, and Fridays.

The French Language was taught to students of the Junior and Sophomore Classes, in two Sections. One hour a day, three days in the week, throughout the year, was devoted to each Section. The instruction was given by translation from text-books, written exercises, and practice in speaking at each recitation.

Instruction was given in German by translation from German into English and from English into German, the text-books used being Göthe's "Faust" and Follen's "German Reader." The Instructor has paid especial attention to grounding the students thoroughly in the elements of the language, and has met his class one evening in each week for practice in conversation.

The students in Spanish and Italian from the Senior and Junior Classes recited in two Sections three times a week during the year. Instruction was given by translation from text-books, and by written exercises.

---

* In Spanish and Italian the instruction is given by Professor Lowell.

Instruction in Italian was given to one Section of Seniors three times a week during the year, by translation from text-books, written exercises, and practice in speaking.

Professor Lowell delivered Lectures during the First Term of the Academic Year. A class of volunteer students in Italian read Dante with him three times a week during the year.

---

9. MATHEMATICS.

The instruction in this Department was given by Benjamin Peirce, LL.D., Perkins Professor of Astronomy and Mathematics, Charles William Eliot, Assistant Professor of Mathematics and Chemistry, and Edward Pearce, Tutor.

The Freshman Class recited in four sections on four days of the week, Tuesday, Thursday, Friday, and Saturday, throughout the year, from the following text-books; namely, Peirce's Plane and Solid Geometry, Peirce's Algebra, except Chapters IV. and VIII., and Chauvenet's Plane Trigonometry.

The Sophomore Class recited in four sections, on three days in the week, Tuesday, Thursday, and Friday, throughout the year, from the following text-books; namely, Peirce's Spherical Trigonometry, Chapter IV. of Peirce's Algebra, and J. M. Peirce's Analytic Geometry.

Instruction was given to those who elected Mathematics in the Junior and Senior years by Lectures and Recitations, on three days in the week, Monday, Wednesday, and Friday, throughout the year, in the Differential, Imaginary, Integral, and Residual Calculuses and the Calculus of Quaternions, and in the Mathematical Theory of Mechanics and Astronomy.

---

10. PHYSICS.

During the past academical year, instruction in this Department was conducted by Joseph Lovering, A.M., Hollis Professor of Mathematics and Natural Philosophy.

The whole Junior Class attended recitations three times a week during the First and Second Terms; and read Herschel's Outlines of Astronomy and Lardner's Course of Natural Philosophy. This Class was examined at the end of the Second Term in both books. The examination was both oral and written.

Each Class was divided into three Divisions; and each Division remained with the instructor one hour at every exercise; in all nine hours a week.

The Senior Class attended a course of twenty-four Lectures on Physics and Experimental Philosophy. The Junior Class attended a similar course of twenty-four Lectures. The whole course, which extends through two years, consists of about sixty Lectures of one hour each; or one Lecture to each Class for every week of both Terms. The subject last year was Mechanics, applied to Solids, Liquids, and Gases, including Optics. These Lectures are always attended by some members of the Scientific and Professional Schools.

---

11. Chemistry and Mineralogy.

The instruction in this Department was given by Josiah P. Cooke, A.M., Erving Professor. During the First Term, the Sophomore Class recited twice a week, from the first half of Stöckhardt's Elements of Chemistry, and attended a course of Experimental Lectures on the Chemistry of the Non-Metallic Elements. During the Second Term, the same Class recited twice a week, from the remainder of the same book, and attended a course of about thirty Lectures on the Chemistry of the Metallic Elements.

The Junior Class recited twice a week from a work on Chemical Physics prepared by the Professor expressly for their use. The portion of the book studied was that relating to Mechanics, Hydrostatics, and Pneumatics.

---

12. Natural History.

This Department was under the care of Asa Gray, M.D., Fisher Professor of Natural History.

Throughout the Second Term the whole Sophomore Class were instructed in Vegetable Physiology and Morphology, by recitations from Gray's Botanical Text-Book, with informal Lectures, microscopical demonstrations, and written examinations. These exercises were attended by the Class, in three Sections, twice a week, on Tuesdays and Thursdays.

A course of Lectures upon Geographical and Systematic Botany, consisting of two Lectures per week throughout the Term, was delivered to those students of the Junior Class who elected the study. These Lectures were attended by about fifty Juniors and a few Scientific Students. From the middle of May to the end of the Term, private practical lessons were given by the Professor, twice a week, to thirty members of the Class, who chose to avail themselves of the privilege.

The course of Lectures on Geology, delivered by Professor Agassiz during the First Term, and that upon Zoölogy during the Second Term, are open to members of the Senior Class.

---

13. ANATOMY AND PHYSIOLOGY.

A course of twenty-three Lectures on the Anatomy and Physiology of Animals was delivered during the First Term to the members of the Senior Class, by Jeffries Wyman, M.D., Hersey Professor of Anatomy. The Lectures were given on Tuesdays and Thursdays, at 12 M., in the anatomical lecture-room in Boylston Hall.

II. PROFESSIONAL SCHOOLS.

1. DIVINITY SCHOOL.

The Divinity School was under the superintendence of the Rev. Convers Francis, D.D., Parkman Professor of Pulpit Eloquence and the Pastoral Care; the Rev. George R. Noyes, D.D., Hancock Professor of Hebrew and other Oriental Languages, and Dexter Lecturer on Sacred Literature; the Rev. Frederick H. Hedge, D.D., Professor of Ecclesiastical History; and Rev. George E. Ellis, D.D., Professor of Systematic Theology.

The course of instruction in the Divinity School occupies three years. The School consists of three Classes; the Junior, Middle, and Senior.

Each Professor attends exercises with each of the Classes through the year. The course of instruction is divided between them as follows. To the Parkman Professor are allotted the branches of Natural Religion, Christian Ethics, and Practical Divinity, Church Polity, the Composition and Delivery of Sermons, and the Duties of the Pastoral Office, together with several Exercises of a miscellaneous character. To the Hancock Professor, the Principles of Criticism and Interpretation, the Criticism and Interpretation of the Old and the New Testaments, and the Hebrew Language. The Professor of Ecclesiastical History and the Professor of Systematic Theology give instruction in the branches of Theology which their titles designate.

The members of the Senior Class preach on Sunday evening during part of the year in one of the churches of this city.

There is also a weekly exercise in extemporaneous speaking, attended by the whole School.

The present number of students (December, 1860) is 22. They come from the States of Vermont, New Hampshire, Maine, Massachusetts, New York, Pennsylvania, Ohio, and Indiana; and those of them who are graduates, from Dartmouth, Bowdoin, Amherst, Harvard, and Antioch Colleges, and from the Philadelphia Central High School.

2. LAW SCHOOL.

During the Academic Year 1859 – 60, the Law School has continued under the superintendence of Joel Parker, LL.D., Royall Professor of Law, Theophilus Parsons, LL.D., Dane Professor of Law, and Emory Washburn, LL.D., University Professor of Law.

The Royall Professor has delivered Lectures upon the Law of Bailments, Corporations, Pleading, Constitutional Law and the Jurisprudence of the United States, and Equity Jurisprudence, Pleading, and Evidence.

The Dane Professor has delivered Lectures upon Blackstone's Commentaries, Kent's Commentaries, the Law of Shipping and Admiralty, the Law of Bills and Notes, and the Law of Partnership.

The University Professor has delivered Lectures upon the Domestic Relations, upon Bankruptcy, Conflict of Laws, and the Law of Sales, and the Law of Real Property.

There have been no new arrangements in relation to the organization of the School or the course of instruction.

Ten Lectures are delivered in each week, generally from text-books designated; and in the course of the Lectures examinations are made, by inquiry of the students as to cases or principles presented to them in connection with the subject-matter of the Lecture. The Faculty continue this method of examination, being convinced that no other would meet so satisfactorily the wants of the School.

A Moot Court has been held each week by one of the Professors; and continued experience strengthens the confidence of the Faculty and the students in the great utility of these courts. That they must be especially useful to the students engaged in them as counsel is obvious. But they are almost equally profitable to others who investigate the questions presented, and indeed to all who attend them, and make use of the opportunities they offer to learn to take notes readily and accurately.

Clubs for discussion and debate, and for the argument of cases, have been continued by the students. The Faculty regard them as eminently useful, and provide for them all the facilities and encouragement in their power.

Prizes for Dissertations have been awarded as before; with the usual strong commendation of the essays by the Committee.

The average number of students attending in the course of the year was one hundred and sixty-one. They came from twenty-six of the United States, the District of Columbia, the Isthmus of Panama, and France.

The degree of LL.B. was conferred at Commencement upon sixty-two students.

3. MEDICAL SCHOOL.

This School was under the superintendence of

D. Humphreys Storer, M.D., Professor of Midwifery and Medical Jurisprudence;

J. B. S. Jackson, M.D., Shattuck Professor of Morbid Anatomy;

Henry I. Bowditch, M.D., Jackson Professor of Clinical Medicine;

George C. Shattuck, Hersey Professor of the Theory and Practice of Physic;

Oliver W. Holmes, M.D., Parkman Professor of Anatomy and Physiology;

Henry J. Bigelow, M.D., Professor of Surgery;

Edward H. Clarke, M.D., Professor of Materia Medica;

John Bacon, M.D., University Professor of Chemistry.

The Medical School was conducted by the above-named Professors, at the Medical College in North Grove Street, Boston. The instruction was given by Courses of Lectures, delivered by the several Professors in their respective departments. The Lectures begin annually on the first Wednesday in November, and continue four months, or seventeen weeks. The students also attend the practice of the Hospital.

The number of students attending Medical Lectures in the session of 1859–60 was 191.

The above School is devoted exclusively to Medical Students, Undergraduates not being permitted to attend.

4. LAWRENCE SCIENTIFIC SCHOOL.

This institution was under the superintendence of

Louis Agassiz, LL.D., Lawrence Professor of Zoölogy and Geology;

Benjamin Peirce, LL.D., Perkins Professor of Astronomy and Mathematics ;

Asa Gray, M.D., Fisher Professor of Natural History ;

Joseph Lovering, A.M., Hollis Professor of Mathematics and Natural Philosophy ;

Jeffries Wyman, M.D., Hersey Professor of Anatomy ;

Henry L. Eustis, A.M., Lawrence Professor of Engineering ;

Eben Norton Horsford, A.M., Rumford Professor, and Lecturer on the Application of the Sciences to the Useful Arts, and Dean of the Faculty ;

Josiah P. Cooke, A.M., Erving Professor of Chemistry and Mineralogy.

The course of instruction embraces systematic practical exercises in the several Laboratories of Professors Agassiz, Wyman, Gray, and Horsford ; instruction in Engineering under the direction of Professor Eustis ; occasional excursions to localities and manufacturing establishments of scientific interest in the neighborhood ; recitations ; and Lectures.

The Lectures are as follows : —

On Geology, and on the Structure and Classification of the Animal Kingdom, by Professor Agassiz, between forty and forty-five Lectures each Term. Scientific excursions are made about once a fortnight.

On the Differential Calculus, twice a week, thirty Lectures ; and on Analytical Mechanics, three times a week, forty-five Lectures, by Professor Peirce.

The Lectures were attended by several members of the Scientific and Law Schools, and by the Undergraduates.

The number of Special Students in all branches of science was ninety-seven, exclusive of the members of the other Professional Schools, and of the Undergraduates, who attended the Scientific Lectures.

---

5. ASTRONOMICAL OBSERVATORY.

During the past year the Astronomical Observatory has been under the superintendence of George P. Bond, A.M., Director of the Observatory.

The Observatory was not founded for the purpose of giving elementary instruction in Astronomy and the kindred sciences, but to furnish accurate systematic observations of the heavenly bodies, and to co-operate in other investigations for the public good. It is, however, open to persons wishing to enter upon a thorough course of instruction in Practical Astronomy.

6. *Museum of Comparative Zoölogy.*

The Museum has been under the superintendence of Louis Agassiz, Professor of Geology and Zoölogy in the Lawrence Scientific School. The lectures and instruction in his department of the Scientific School have been given at the Museum, where the special students have been employed in their several branches of study, under the direction of the Professor.

II.

SUMMARY OF UNDERGRADUATES, PROFESSIONAL STUDENTS, AND RESIDENT GRADUATES, AT THE BEGINNING OF THE ACADEMICAL YEAR 1859 – 60.

Undergraduates.

Seniors	107
Juniors	84
Sophomores	112
Freshmen	128
	431

Professional Students and Resident Graduates.

Theological Students	21
Law Students	166
Students attending Medical Lectures	140
Special Students in the Lawrence Scientific School	75
Resident Graduates	15
	417

Total	848
Deduct repetitions	9
Total	839

III.

Academic Honors and Prizes for the Year 1859 – 60.

1. *Deturs.*

The following students received presents of books called "Deturs," from the donation of Edward Hopkins, at the commencement of their Junior or Sophomore year.

JUNIORS.

James Vila Blake,	Samuel Cushman Haven,
John Hoag Dillingham,	Charles Hume Noyes.

SOPHOMORES.

Frederic Baylies Allen,	Henry Lunt,
George Lewis Baxter,	Francis Alexander Marden,
Frederic Brooks,	George Shattuck Morison,
Moses Grant Daniell,	William Nichols,
Edward Bangs Drew,	Roscoe Palmer Owen,
Benj. Thompson Frothingham,	William Henry Palmer,
Joseph Anthony Gillett,	Thomas Bellows Peck,
Frederic Thomas Greenhalgh,	William Low Pillsbury,
Thomas Robinson Harris,	Henry Newton Sheldon,
Henry Fitch Jenks,	Edward Gray Stetson,
William Furness Jenks,	Michael Shepard Webb,
Arthur Mason Knapp,	Charles Stuart Weld,
Arthur Lincoln,	Edmund Souder Wheeler,
William Linder,	William Augustus White.
Josiah Lombard,	

---

2. *Exhibition, October 18th, 1859.*

SENIOR PERFORMANCES.

George Everett Adams,	A Dissertation.
William Sumner Appleton,	A Disquisition.
Henry Austin Clapp,	A Dissertation.
Edward Crosby Johnson,	An Essay.

Silas Dean Presbrey,	A Disquisition.
Henry George Spaulding,	An English Oration.
George Willis Warren,	A Dissertation.
Stephen Minot Weld,	An Essay.
Edmund Wetmore,	A Latin Oration.
George Henry Whittemore,	A Disquisition.
William Converse Wood,	Do.
Calvin Milton Woodward,	An Essay.

JUNIOR PERFORMANCES.

Leonard Case Alden,	A Latin Version.
Henry Pickering Bowditch,	An English Version.
Jeremiah Wesley Boyden,	A Greek Dialogue.
Lewis Stackpole Dabney,	A Latin Dialogue.
Wendell Phillips Garrison,	A Greek Version.
Joseph Bradford Hardon,	A Latin Dialogue.
Joseph Hetherington McDaniels,	An English Version.
George Hart Mumford,	A Greek Dialogue.
William Henry Pettee,	An English Version.
Henry Pickering,	Do.
James Kent Stone,	Do.
Richard Stone,	A Latin Version.

---

3. *Exhibition, May* 1st, 1860.

SENIOR PERFORMANCES.

Henry Freeman Allen,	A Dissertation.
William Gardner Colburn,	A Disquisition.
Thomas Bayley Fox,	A Dissertation.
William Eliot Furness,	Do.
William Channing Gannett,	A Latin Oration.
James Haughton,	A Disquisition.
Julius Sedgwick Hood,	An English Oration.
Charles Alfred Humphreys,	A Disquisition.
John Torrey Morse,	Do.
Hersey Goodwin Palfrey,	Do.
Charles Appleton Phillips,	Do.
Lewis William Tappan,	A Dissertation.
James Bryant Walker,	A Disquisition.
George Gill Wheelock,	An English Oration.

JUNIOR PERFORMANCES.

Stephen Goodhue Emerson,	A Greek Version.
Frank Warren Hackett,	An English Version.
Oliver Wendell Holmes,	Do.
David Francis Lincoln,	A Latin Version.

Scollay Parker,	A Latin Version.
Samuel Dunn Phillips,	A Latin Dialogue.
John Ritchie,	A Greek Version.
Charles Christie Salter,	An English Version.
Herbert Sleeper,	A Greek Dialogue.
William Franklin Snow,	Do.
James Putnam Walker,	An English Version.
James Edward Wright,	A Latin Dialogue.

---

4. *Commencement, July 18th, 1860.*

Henry George Spaulding,	An English Oration.
Julius Sedgwick Hood,	Do.
William Eliot Furness,	Do.
George Willis Warren,	Do.
Edmund Wetmore,	Do.
George Gill Wheelock,	Do.
Henry Austin Clapp,	Do.
George Everett Adams,	Do.
William Channing Gannett,	Do.
Thomas Bayley Fox,	A Dissertation.
William Gardner Colburn,	Do.
George Henry Whittemore,	Do.
Lewis William Tappan,	Do.
Henry Freeman Allen,	A Salutatory Oration.
Hersey Goodwin Palfrey,	A Dissertation.
James Bryant Walker,	Do.
William Converse Wood,	Do.
Charles Appleton Phillips,	Do.
James Haughton,	Do.
James Champlin Fernald,	A Disquisition.
Silas Dean Presbrey,	Do.
Edward Crosby Johnson,	Do.
Calvin Milton Woodward,	Do.
George Brooks Young,	Do.
Albert Blodgett Weymouth,	Do.
Charles Alfred Humphreys,	Do.
John Torrey Morse,	Do.
Stephen William Driver,	Do.
William Sumner Appleton,	Do.
John Treadwell Cole,	An Essay.
Henry Bruce Scott,	Do.
John William Stearns,	Do.
William Hooper Adams,	Do.
Charles James Mills,	Do.
Samuel Gilbert Webber,	Do.

Francis Minot Weld,	An Essay.
Joseph Shippen,	Do.
James Augustus Towle,	Do.
Stephen Minot Weld,	Do.
Charles Adams Horne,	Do.
Henry Leonard,	Do.
Henry Hinckley,	Do.
Addison Gilbert Smith,	Do.

5. *Prize Dissertations in the Law School.*

CHARLES FOLSOM WALCOTT, a First Prize.
THOMAS KINNICUTT, a Second Prize.
ROBERT DICKSON SMITH, a First Prize.
ALFRED LEWIS EDWARDS, a Second Prize.

6. *Bowdoin Prize Dissertations.*

Resident Graduate.
HENRY WALKER FROST.

Class of 1860.

JAMES CHAMPLIN FERNALD, a First Prize.
WILLIAM GARDNER COLBURN, a Second Prize.

Present Senior Class.
GEORGE HART MUMFORD, a First Prize.
JAMES KENT STONE, a Second Prize.

7. *Bowdoin Prizes for Latin and Greek Composition.*
Class of 1860.
HENRY GEORGE SPAULDING, Greek Prose.

Present Senior Class.
JOHN PRENTISS HOPKINSON, Latin Verse.

8. *Boylston Prizes for Elocution.*
First Prizes.

THOMAS BAYLEY FOX, of the Graduating Class.
JAMES VILA BLAKE, of the present Junior Class.
Second Prizes.
EDWARD AUGUSTUS CROWNINSHIELD, of the present Senior
Class.
WESLEY CALEB SAWYER, of the present Senior Class.
WILLIAM FRANKLIN SNOW, of the present Senior Class.

9. *Harvard Mathematical Prizes.*

CALVIN MILTON WOODWARD, of the Class of 1860.
CHARLES APPLETON PHILLIPS, of the Class of 1860.

---

10. *Degrees in Course.*

Bachelors of Arts of the Class of 1860 - - - - -	102
Bachelors of Arts of former Classes - - - -	5
Masters of Arts of the Class of 1857 - - - -	17
Masters of Arts of former Classes - - - -	17
Graduates in the Divinity School - - - - -	14
Doctors of Medicine - - - - - - - -	52
Bachelors of Laws - - - - - - - -	62
Bachelors in Science - - - - - - -	5
Total - - - - - -	231

---

11. *Honorary Degrees.*

Masters of Arts.

WILLIAM MITCHELL, of Nantucket.
JOHN GREENLEAF WHITTIER, of Amesbury.
CHARLES FREDERIC BRADFORD, of Roxbury.
GEORGE ADAM SCHMITT, of Cambridge.
REINHOLD SOLGER, of Roxbury.
GARDINER HOWLAND SHAW, of Boston.
GRINDALL REYNOLDS, of Concord.
THOMAS BALDWIN THAYER, of Boston.
WILLIAM HENRY RYDER, of Illinois.
JAMES SULLIVAN AMORY, of Boston.

Doctors of Divinity.

Rev. ALFRED LEE, of Delaware.
Rev. THOMAS HILL, President of Antioch College.
Rev. WILLIAM BROCK, of London, England.

Doctors of Laws.

JAMES WALKER, of Cambridge.
WILLIAM BRADFORD REED, of Pennsylvania.
JOHN LOTHROP MOTLEY, of Boston.
LORD LYONS, British Minister at Washington.

IV.

The following Tables exhibit the times and subjects of the Recitations and Lectures for every Class, in each Term of the Academical Year.

Tabular View of the Exercises during the First Term of 1859–60.

Italics indicate Elective Studies.

MONDAY

Class.	8—9.	9—10.	10—11.	11—12.	12—1.	4—5.	5—6.
Fr.	I. Latin. IV. Greek.	II. Latin. III. Greek.	IV. Elocution.	I. Relig. Instruction.	II. Relig. Instruction. / Themes.	I. Greek. IV. Latin.	II. Greek. III. Latin.
Soph.	I. Greek. IV. Latin.	II. Greek. III. Latin.	*German. Math.* / *Latin.*	*French.* / *German. Italian. Math.*	*Chem. French. Span.* / *German. Greek.*	I. Latin. IV. Greek.	II. Latin. III. Greek.
Jun.	I. Chem. III. Physics.	II. Physics.				III. Chemistry.	I. Physics. II. Chem.
Sen.	I. Philos. III. Rhet.	II. Rhetoric.				III. Philosophy.	I. Rhet. II. Philos.

TUESDAY

Class.	8—9.	9—10.	10—11.	11—12.	12—1.	4—5.	5—6.
Fr.	I. Latin. IV. Mat.	II. Latin. III. Math.	III. Elocution.	I. Math. IV. Greek.	II. Math. III. Greek.	I. Greek. IV. Latin.	II. Greek. III. Latin.
Soph.	I. Rhet. III. Chem.	II. Chemistry.		IV. Mathematics.	I. Chem. III. Math.	I. Math. II. Rhetoric.	II. Mat. III. Rhetoric.
Jun.	I. Latin. II. Greek.	III. Greek.	*Geology.**	Physics.*	Declamation.	II. Latin.	I. Greek. III. Latin.
Sen.	I. Philos. III. History.	II. History.		Forensics.	Anatomy.* or Math.*	III. Philos. I. History.	II. History.

WEDNESDAY

Class.	8—9.	9—10.	10—11.	11—12.	12—1.	4—5.	5—6.
Fr.	I. Latin. IV. Greek.	II. Latin. III. Greek.	II. Elocution.	I. Relig. Instruction.	I. Elo. II. Relig. Inst.	I. Greek. IV. Latin.	II. Greek. III. Latin.
Soph.	I. Greek. IV. Latin.	II. Greek. III. Latin.	Latin or Greek. / *German. Math.* / *Latin.*	*French.* / *German. Italian. Math.*	*Chem. French. Span.* / *German. Greek.*	I. Latin. IV. Greek.	II. Latin. III. Greek.
Jun.	I. Chem. III. Physics.	II. Physics.				III. Chemistry.	I. Physics. II. Chem.
Sen.	I. Philos. III. History.	II. History.				III. Philos. I. History.	II. Philos. I. History.

THURSDAY

Class.	8—9.	9—10.	10—11.	11—12.	12—1.	4—5.	5—6.
Fr.	I. Latin. IV. Mat.	II. Lat. III. Math.		I. Math. IV. Greek.	II. Math. III. Greek.	I. Greek. IV. Latin.	II. Greek. III. Latin.
Soph.	I. Rhet. III. Chem.	II. Chemistry.		IV. Mathematics.	I. Chem. III. Math.	I. Math. II. Rhetoric.	II. Math. III. Rhet.
Jun.	I. Latin. II. Greek.	III. Greek.	*Geology.**	Themes.	Greek Literature.*	II. Latin.	I. Greek. III. Latin.
Sen.	I. Philos. III. Hist.	II. History.		Physics.*	Anatomy.* or Math.*	III. Philos. I. History.	II. Philos. I. History.

FRIDAY

Class.	8—9.	9—10.	10—11.	11—12.	12—1.	4—5.	5—6.
Fr.	I. Greek. IV. Math.	II. Greek. III. Math.	I. Elocution.	I. Comp. IV. Greek.	II. Comp. III. Greek.	I. Math. IV. Comp.	II. Math. III. Comp.
Soph.	I. Gr. II. Elo. IV. Mat.	II. Gr III. M. IV. El.	*German. Math.* / *Latin.*	*French.* / *German. Italian. Math.*	Chemistry.* / *Chem. French. Span.* / *German. Greek.*	I. Ma. III. Elo. IV. Lat.	II. Math. III. Latin.
Jun.	I. Latin. III. Physics.	II. Physics.				II. Latin.	I. Greek. III. Latin.
Sen.	I. History.‡	II. History.‡				*Modern Literature.**	I. Physics. III. Latin.

SATURDAY

Class.	8—9.	9—10.	10—11.	11—12.	12—1.	4—5.	5—6.
Fr.	I. and II. Math.†	III. and IV. Math.†					
Soph.	I. Latin. IV. Greek.	II. Latin. III. Greek.					
Jun.	II. and III. Greek.†	I. Greek.†					
Sen.	I. Rhetoric.‡	II. Rhetoric.‡					

* Lectures.   † Half-hour Recitations.   ‡ In *two* divisions.

NOTE. — During the First Term, Morning Prayers will begin at a quarter before seven o'clock, and the hour of dinner will be one o'clock, until the Thanksgiving recess. After the Thanksgiving recess, Morning Prayers will begin at a quarter before eight o'clock, all the Morning Exercises will be attended one hour later than the time indicated in the Table, and the hour of dinner will be two o'clock.

Tabular View of the Exercises during the Second Term of 1859 – 60.

Italics indicate Elective Studies.

	Class.	8 — 9.	9 — 10.	10 — 11.	11 — 12.	12 — 1.	4 — 5.	5 — 6.
MOND.	Fr.	I. Latin. IV. History.	II. Lat. III. History.	I. Elocution.	I. History. IV. Greek.	II. Hist. III. Greek.	I. Greek. IV. Latin.	II. Greek. III. Latin.
	Soph.	I. Greek. IV. Latin.	II. Greek. III. Latin.	*German. Italian. Math.*	*French.*	English Literature.*	I. Latin. IV. Greek.	II. Latin. III. Greek.
	Jun.	I. Rhet. III. Physics.	II. Physics.	*Latin.*	*German. Italian.*	*Chem. French. Span.*	III. Rhetoric.	I. Physics. II. Rhet.
	Sen.	I. History. III. Philos.	II. Philosophy.		*Italian. Math.*	*German. Greek.*	III. History.	I. Philos. II. History.
TUES.	Fr.	I. Latin. IV. Math.	II. L. III. Mat. IV. El.	II. Elocution.	I. Math. IV. Greek.	II. Math. III. Greek.	I. Greek. IV. Latin.	II. Greek. III. Latin.
	Soph.	II. Chem. IV. Math.	I. Chem. III. Math.		I. Math. III. Elocu.	II. Math. III. Botany.	II. Botany.	I. Botany. III. Chem.
	Jun.	I. Greek. II. Latin.	III. Latin.	*Botany.**	Physics.*	Declamation.	II. Greek.	I. Latin. III. Greek.
	Sen.	I. History. III. Philos.	II. Philosophy.		Forensics.	Zoölogy.*	III. History.	I. Philos. II. History.
WEDN.	Fr.	I. Latin. IV. History.	II. Latin. III. History.	Latin or Greek.	I. Hist. IV. Greek.	II. Hist. III. Greek.	I. Greek. IV. Latin.	II. Greek. III. Latin.
	Soph.	I. Greek. IV. Latin.	II. Greek. III. Latin.	*German. Math.*	*French.*	Themes.	I. Latin. IV. Greek.	II. Latin. III. Greek.
	Jun.	I. Rhet. III. Physics.	II. Physics.	*Latin.*	*German. Italian.*	*Chem. French. Span.*	III. Rhetoric.	I. Physics. II. Rhet.
	Sen.	I. History. III. Philos.	II. Philosophy.		*Italian. Math.*	*German. Greek.*	III. History.	I. Philos. II. History.
THUR.	Fr.	I. Latin. IV. Math.	I.El. II.Lat. III.Math.	III. Elocution.	I. Math. IV. Greek.	II. Math. III. Greek.	I. Greek. IV. Latin.	II. Greek. III. Latin.
	Soph.	II. Chem. IV. Math.	I. Chem. III. Math.		I. Mathematics.	II. Math. III. Botany.	II. Botany.	I. Botany. III. Chem.
	Jun.	I. Greek. II. Latin.	III. Latin.	*Botany.**		Themes.	II. Greek.	I. Latin. III. Greek.
	Sen.	I. History. III. Philos.	II. Philosophy.		Physics.*	Zoölogy.*	III. History.	I. Philos. II. History.
FRID.	Fr.	I. Comp. IV. Math.	II. Comp. III. Math.	II. Elocution.	I. Greek. IV. Comp.	II. Greek. III. Comp.	I. Math. IV. Greek.	I. Math. III. Greek.
	Soph.	I. Greek. IV. Math.	II.Gr. III.Mat. IV.El.	*German. Math.*	*French.*	Chemistry.*	I. Math. IV. Latin.	II. Math. III. Latin.
	Jun.	I. Greek. III. Physics.	I. Physics.	*Latin.*	*German. Italian.*	*Chem. French. Span.*	II. Greek.	I. Physics. III. Greek.
	Sen.	II. Ethics.‡	I. Ethics.‡		*Italian. Math.*	*German. Greek.*		History or Philos.*
SATUR.	Fr.	I. and II. Math.†	III. and IV. Math.†					
	Soph.	I. Latin. IV. Greek.	II. Latin. III. Greek.					
	Jun.	II. and III. Latin.†	I. Latin.†					
	Sen.	II. Ethics.‡	I. Ethics.‡					

* Lectures. † Half-hour Recitations. ‡ In two divisions.

LECTURES TO UNDERGRADUATES.

First Term.

SENIOR CLASS.

Modern Literature, — PROFESSOR LOWELL, Friday, at 4 o'clock, in Harvard Hall.

Anatomy, — PROFESSOR WYMAN, Tuesday and Thursday, at 10 o'clock, in Boylston Hall.

Geology, — PROFESSOR AGASSIZ, to the Lawrence Scientific School, Tuesday and Thursday, at 12 o'clock, in Boylston Hall.

Mathematics, — PROFESSOR PEIRCE, Tuesday and Thursday, at 10 o'clock, in Harvard Hall.

Statics and Hydrostatics, — PROFESSOR LOVERING, Thursday, at 11 o'clock, in No. 2 University Hall.

JUNIOR CLASS.

Greek Literature, — PROFESSOR FELTON, Thursday, at 12 o'clock, in Harvard Hall.

Statics and Hydrostatics, — PROFESSOR LOVERING, Tuesday, at 11 o'clock, in No. 2 University Hall.

SOPHOMORE CLASS.

Chemistry, — PROFESSOR COOKE, Friday, at 12 o'clock, in Boylston Hall.

Second Term.

SENIOR CLASS.

Philosophy and History, — PROFESSOR BOWEN or PROFESSOR TORREY, Friday, at 5 o'clock, in Harvard Hall.

Modern Literature, — PROFESSOR LOWELL, Thursday, at 4 o'clock, in Harvard Hall.

Dynamics, Optics, and Acoustics, — PROFESSOR LOVERING, Thursday, at 11 o'clock, in No. 2 University Hall.

Zoölogy, — PROFESSOR AGASSIZ, to the Lawrence Scientific School, Tuesday and Thursday, at 12 o'clock, in the Zoölogical Museum.

JUNIOR CLASS.

Dynamics, Optics, and Acoustics, — PROFESSOR LOVERING, Tuesday, at 11 o'clock, in No. 2 University Hall.

Botany, — PROFESSOR GRAY, Tuesday and Thursday, at 10 o'clock, in Holden Chapel.

V.

COMMITTEES OF EXAMINATION FOR THE YEAR 1860.

GENERAL COMMITTEES.

1. *Committee for Visiting the University.*

His Excellency, the Governor,
His Honor, the Lieutenant-Governor,
The President of the Senate,
The Speaker of the House of Representatives,
The Secretary of the Board of Education,

The Secretary of the Overseers,
Hon. Marcus Morton, LL.D.
Hon. Josiah G. Abbott,
Rev. Rodney A. Miller,
Rev. Baron Stow, D.D.
Rev. Thomas Worcester, D.D.
Rev. Thomas B. Thayer,
Rev. Lorenzo R. Thayer.

2. *On the Library, &c.*

Hon. Emory Washburn, LL.D.
J. G. Whittier, Esq.
Rev. P. B. Haughwaut,
Richard S. Spofford, M. D.
Rev. William Jenks, D.D.
Charles Folsom, Esq.
George Livermore, Esq.
Samuel F. Haven, Esq.
Charles Deane, Esq.
William Gray, Esq.
Franklin Haven, Esq.
Theodore R. Jencks, Esq.
Hon. Joseph T. Buckingham,
Hon. William T. Davis,
Hon. George D. Wells,

Rev. John P. Cleaveland, D.D.
Rev. Richard M. Hodges,
Elijah B. Stoddard, Esq.
Henry A. Whitney, Esq.
William F. Poole, Esq.
Henry G. Denny, Esq.
Samuel A. Green, M.D.
J. Wingate Thornton, Esq.
Hon. Henry K. Oliver,
Edward Jarvis, M.D.
Hon. David K. Hitchcock,
William D. Ticknor, Esq.
James A. Dix, Esq.
Isaac C. Taber, Esq.
Josiah Bartlett, M.D.

3. *On the Treasurer's Accounts.*

Hon. Jacob Sleeper,
Hon. Julius Rockwell,
Hon. George Morey,
Joel Hayden, Esq.

William Amory, Esq.
William Minot, Jr., Esq.
Matthew Howland, Esq.
Hon. Nathaniel Silsbee.

SPECIAL COMMITTEES.

1. *For Examination in the Greek Language.*

Hon. Stephen M. Weld,
Rev. P. B. Haughwaut,
Hon. George Morey,
Samuel H. Taylor, LL.D.
Epes S. Dixwell, Esq.
Charles K. Dillaway, Esq.
John Codman, Esq.
Rev. Rufus Ellis,
James C. Merrill, Esq.
Rev. Horatio B. Hackett, D.D.
Henry A. Johnson, Esq.
John Ruggles, Esq.
John Noble, Esq.
William A. Crafts, Esq.
Henry C. Kimball, Esq.
Rev. Theodore Tebbets,
Rev. Daniel Steel,
J. L. Stackpole, Esq.

2. *For Examination in the Latin Language.*

Henry B. Wheelwright, Esq.
Abner J. Phipps, Esq.
Charles Beck, P.D.
Francis Gardner, Esq.
Thomas Bulfinch, Esq.
Rev. James I. T. Coolidge,
Rev. Charles H. Brigham,
Rev. Gilbert Haven,
Warren Tilton, Esq.
Moses H. Day, Esq.
Rev. Samuel B. Cruft,
Z. K. Pangborn, Esq.
Henry W. Haynes, Esq.
Hon. Ozias C. Pitkin,
Rev. Edward B. Otheman,
Edwin Wright, Esq.
William E. Fuller, Esq.
Henry L. Hallett, Esq.
Loring Lothrop, Esq.
David H. Coolidge, Esq.

3. *For Examination in the Modern Languages.*

Rev. A. P. Mason, D.D.
Rev. Samuel F. Smith, D.D.
Rev. Edward N. Kirk, D.D.
Rev. William R. Bagnall,
Charles F. Bradford, Esq.
William C. Williamson, Esq.
Rev. Charles C. Shackford,
Rev. William F. Warren,
Hon. G. Washington Warren,
Rev. Frederic W. Holland,
Rev. D. G. Haskins,
Charles D. Homans, M.D.
Calvin Ellis, M.D.
William W. Clapp, Jr., Esq.
William H. Seavey, Esq.
Hon. John S. Sleeper,
Charles A. Chase, Esq.
Charles C. Hobbs, Esq.

4. *For Examination in Rhetoric, Logic, and Grammar.*

Rev. John H. Twombly,
Rev. Austin Phelps, D.D.
Rev. E. O. Haven, D.D.
Rev. Daniel W. Stevens,
Joseph Palmer, M.D.
Joseph Story, Esq.
Ezra Palmer, M.D.
Henry G. Denny, Esq.
Augustus O. Brewster, Esq.
John D. Philbrick, Esq.
D. B. Hager, Esq.
A. P. Stone, Esq.
Rev. Henry M. Dexter,
Rev. Fales H. Newhall,

Rev. H. L. Wayland,
Rev. Horace James,
Rev. W. F. Mallalieu,

Rev. Isaac S. Cushman,
George A. Shaw, Esq.
John S. Holmes, Esq.

5. *For Examination in the Mathematics.*

Rev. John Wayland, D.D.
Philip H. Sears, Esq.
Prof. Joseph Winlock,
J. D. Runkle, Esq.
Chauncey Wright, Esq.
Truman Henry Safford, Esq.
Thomas Sherwin, Esq.
Hon. Charles Hale,

James W. Stone, M.D.
John B. Henck, Esq.
Edwin Clapp, Esq.
Werden Reynolds, Esq.
Marshall Conant, Esq.
Baylies Sanford, Esq.
John S. Keyes, Esq.

6. *For Examination in Intellectual and Moral Philosophy.*

Philip H. Sears, Esq.
Hon. Thomas Russell,
Rev. N. L. Frothingham, D.D.
Rev. Andrew Bigelow, D.D.
Hon. Stephen H. Phillips,
Hon. James M. Usher,
Rev. R. T. S. Lowell,
Rev. John C. Stockbridge, D.D.
Hon. John G. Palfrey, D.D.

Thomas C. Amory, Jr., Esq.
Arthur T. Lyman, Esq.
Francis E. Parker, Esq.
Thornton K. Lothrop, Esq.
Howard P. Arnold, Esq.
Rev. Joseph H. Allen,
Benjamin F. Presbrey, Esq.
James H. Wilder, Esq.

7. *For Examination in Physics.*

Hon. Joseph M. Churchill,
Rev. Frederic A. Whitney,
Hon. Henry K. Oliver,
Charles Demond, Esq.
David Thayer, M.D.
Rev. Andrew Pollard,
George F. Bigelow, M.D.
Rev. Fales H. Newhall,

Rev. Richard Pike,
William R. Ware, Esq.
Joseph R. Webster, M.D.
James Humphrey, Esq.
Samuel B. Noyes, Esq.
Henry Walker, Esq.
William J. Rolfe, Esq.
Hon. Charles B. Hall.

8. *For Examination in History.*

Nathaniel B. Shurtleff, M.D.
Hon. John P. Bigelow,
Rev. Joseph B. Felt, LL.D.
Rev. Milton P. Braman, D.D.
Joseph E. Worcester, LL.D.
Hon. James D. Green,
Hon. Stephen Salisbury,
Hon. Luther V. Bell, LL.D.

Joseph Willard, Esq.
Thomas Aspinwall, Esq.
William Brigham, Esq.
Hon. Lorenzo Sabine,
Hon. Frederic W. Lincoln, Jr.,
Hon. George White.
George W. Tuxbury, Esq.
Nathaniel L. Hooper, Esq.

9. *For Examination in Political Economy and Constitutional Law.*

Francis Bassett, Esq.
Hon. Willard Phillips, LL.D.
Hon. Solomon Lincoln,
Hon. Charles F. Adams,
Hon. Amasa Walker,
Hon. Thomas D. Eliot,
Hon. Samuel E. Sewall,
William Gray, Esq.
Rev. Alonzo H. Quint,
George Fabyan, M.D.
Richard H. Dana, Esq.
Thornton K. Ware, Esq.

10. *For Examination in Chemistry.*

Hon. Elisha Huntington, M.D.
Charles T. Jackson, M.D.
Augustus A. Hayes, M.D.
Benjamin S. Shaw, M.D.
F. S. Ainsworth, M.D.
James R. Nichols, Esq.
James B. Lane, Esq.
Hon. Jabez Fisher,
Rev. J. W. Wellman,
William W. Godding, M.D.
E. K. Sanborn, M.D.
Henry Clarke, M.D.
Hon. William D. Peck, M.D.
Charles G. Came, Esq.

11. *For Examination in Natural History.*

Hon. Thomas Russell,
Nathaniel T. Allen, Esq.
George P. Bradford, Esq.
Thomas M. Brewer, Esq.
Samuel Cabot, Jr., M.D.
J. Eliot Cabot, Esq.
Charles L. Flint, Esq.
Augustus A. Gould, M.D.
Horace Gray, Jr., Esq.
Samuel Kneeland, Jr., M.D.
Theodore Lyman, Esq.
Rev. John L. Russell,
William G. Russell, Esq.
Albion K. Slade, Esq.
Strafford Tenney, Esq.
Henry D. Thoreau, Esq.
Benjamin M. Watson, Esq.
William Wesselhœft, M.D.
Henry Wheatland, M.D.
William W. Wheildon, Esq.

12. *For Visiting the Observatory.*

Hon. William Mitchell,
Hon. Josiah Quincy, LL.D.
Hon. James Savage, LL.D.
Hon. Jared Sparks, LL.D.
Hon. R. C. Winthrop, LL.D.
Robert T. Paine, Esq.
J. Ingersoll Bowditch, Esq.
Henry C. Perkins, M.D.
David Sears, Jr., Esq.

13. *For Visiting the Divinity School.*

Rev. Rollin H. Neale, D.D.
Rev. Jacob M. Manning,
Rev. A. B. Muzzey,
Rev. Ezra S. Gannett, D.D.
Rev. Samuel K. Lothrop, D.D.
Rev. Hosea Ballou, D.D.
Rev. Nathaniel Cogswell,
Rev. Lorenzo R. Thayer,
Rev. Thomas B. Thayer,
Joel Hayden, Esq.

Rev. Irah Chase, D.D.
Rev. John A. Albro, D.D.
Rev. John Pryor, D.D.
Rev. Henry A. Miles, D.D.

Rev. William Newell, D.D.
Rev. Edmund B. Willson,
Rev. R. B. Thurston,
Hon. Daniel A. White, LL.D.

14. *For Visiting the Law School.*

Charles G. Davis, Esq.
Charles P. Curtis, Esq.
William Brigham, Esq.
Hon. Edward Mellen,
Hon. F. W. Dewey,

Hon. Goldsmith F. Bailey,
David H. Mason, Esq.
Richard S. Spofford, Jr., Esq.
Joseph M. Day, Esq.

15. *For Visiting the Medical School.*

Alfred Hitchcock, M.D.
Winslow Lewis, M.D.
J. Mason Warren, M.D.
William J. Dale, M.D.
John Homans, M.D.
Gilman Kimball, M.D.
Benjamin E. Cotting, M.D.

Thomas R. Boutelle, M.D.
Jonas A. Marshall, M.D.
Henry G. Clark, M.D.
Alfred Miller, M.D.
John G. Metcalf, M.D.
Joseph Sargent, M.D.
J. L. S. Thompson, M.D.

16. *For Visiting the Lawrence Scientific School.*

Winslow Lewis, M.D.
Hon. Emory Washburn, LL.D.
Nathaniel B. Shurtleff, M.D.
Hon. John H. Clifford, LL.D.
Jacob Bigelow, LL.D.
James Hayward, Esq.
John M. Fessenden, Esq.
Augustus A. Gould, M.D.

Daniel Treadwell, Esq.
William W. Greenough, Esq.
James Lawrence, Esq.
Ezra Lincoln, Esq.
Capt. B. S. Alexander, U.S.A.
George H. Gay, M.D.
Samuel Cabot, Jr., M.D.
James R. Wellman, M.D.

TREASURER'S STATEMENT.

To the Honorable and Reverend,
THE OVERSEERS OF HARVARD COLLEGE.

GENTLEMEN: — The accompanying accounts show that the disbursements for the year have been $64,423.81, and the income $60,928.52, leaving a deficiency of $3,495.29. The sum of $2,790, included in this deficiency, has been set aside from the income of Factory Stocks paying over six per cent, for an insurance and guaranty fund; leaving to the debit of the yearly account the sum of $705.29.

The sum of fifty thousand dollars has been received from the executors of the late Abbott Lawrence, which completes his endowment of the Scientific School.

A legacy of six thousand dollars has been received from the estate of Miss Mary Osgood of Medford, which is to be held in trust by the Corporation during the lives of three of her relatives; and afterwards the income is to be used for the purchase of books.

The sum of fourteen hundred dollars has been contributed to the Library Fund.*

A graduate of the College, distinguished among other things for his acts of judicious benevolence, has given two thousand dollars for the support of meritorious students who are poor; and he has indicated his intention of establishing a permanent fund for the same purpose.

An increase has been made to the salaries of the officers of instruction and government, amounting to $4,800.

By the extension of the College House over vacant land belonging to the Corporation, and by rebuilding upon the Webb estate in Boston, some increase of income has been made. .

The income of the " Professorship of Natural History " has always been inadequate for the support of that department, and the average yearly reduction of the fund is $600, leaving at the present time, $12,703.

No progress has been made in the separation of the property of the Divinity School from that of the College. The united petition of the Corporation and Overseers to the Legislature was granted in 1858, and a statute was passed authorizing the College to resign its control of this School and its funds. By the same act the Supreme

---

* By Henry A. Whitney, $500 ; Sundry Graduates, by H. G. Denny, $600 ; James Savage, $100 ; J. S. & J. J. Higginson, $100 ; Sidney Bartlett, $100.

Judicial Court was authorized, on petition of the Corporation, to appoint another Trustee, and to transfer the funds. Such a petition was forthwith presented, but it has neither been granted nor refused by the Court.

Respectfully submitted by

Your obedient servant,

AMOS A. LAWRENCE,

Treasurer.

November 26, 1860.

GENERAL STATEMENT OF RECEIPTS AND
HARVARD COLLEGE, FOR THE

Income.

Interest received on Notes and Mortgages, . .	$ 37,480.80	
Jona. Phillips's Donation (mortgage), . .	600.00	
Baring Brothers & Co., and gain in account,	44.82	
New York Central Railroad Bonds, . .	660.00	
City of Albany Stock, ...	360.00	
Philadelphia and Reading Railroad Bonds, .	120.00	
Trustees of Count Rumford, Paris, . .	577.52	
Edward Hopkins's Donation, . . .	130.00	
Gray Fund for Zoölogical Museum, . .	3,000.00	
" " " Collection of Engravings, .	647.92	
		$ 43,621.06
Dividends on Stock.		
Boston Bank, ...	1,176.00	
Merchants' "	300.00	
Fitchburg "	168.00	
New England "	210.00	
Charles River "	480.00	
Massachusetts "	192.00	
Merrimack Manufacturing Co., . . .	1,700.00	
Cocheco " " . . .	940.00	
Atlantic Mills " " . . .	1,320.00	
Boston -- . . .	600.00	
Great Falls " -- . .	198.00	
Stark -- . . .	1,530.00	
Amoskeag " -- . .	1,080.00	
Appleton	500.00	
Hamilton . . .	400.00	
Massachusetts " . . .	450.00	
Suffolk . . .	450.00	
Manchester " " . .	300.00	
Pacific " " . . .	2,200.00	
Pittsfield and North Adams Railroad, . .	300.00	
Western " .	400.00	
		14,894.00
Appleton Chapel Fund, Rent of Pews, ...	. .	864.00
Annuities. — John Glover's, ...	16.67	
Wm. Pennoyer's, . . .	154.64	
		171.31
Gymnasium. — Charged to Students, ...	. .	1,890.00
Rents. — Houses and Lands, in Cambridge, . .	6,151.34	
Webb Estate, in Boston, . .	3,800.00	
		9,951.34
Atlantic Mills, 3 shares sold, ...	.	3,000.00
Term Bills, charged to Undergraduates for Instruction,	22,978.50	
Rent, and Care of Rooms and Lecture-Rooms, ...	7,256.50	
Advanced Standing, . . .	507.50	
		30,742.50
Amount carried forward, ...	.	$ 105,134.21

No. I.

DISBURSEMENTS BY THE TREASURER OF YEAR ENDING AUGUST 31, 1860.

Expenses.

Paid to Account of

Salaries and Grants in the Academic Department, . .		$42,695.00
W. T. Richardson's Bills for Fuel charged to Students in Term Bills, ...	$6,648.72	
John Bartlett's and Sever & Francis's Bills for Text-Books charged to Students in Term Bills, . .	5,065.78	
Cambridge Gas Co.'s Bills for Gas charged to Students in Term Bills, ...	944.58	
		12,659.08
Income of Beneficiary Fund paid to Undergraduates,	985.00	
" Saltonstall Scholarships " "	180.00	
" Alford " "	25.00	
" Abbot " "	100.00	
" Class of 1814, " "	114.00	
" Shattuck, " "	600.00	
" Pennoyer's " "	150.00	
" Edward Hopkins's Donation, for "Deturs,"	133.25	
		2,287.25
" James Bowdoin's Legacy, for Prizes and for Advertising, ...	260.00	
" Ward N. Boylston's Donation, Prizes for Elocution, ...	60.00	
" Subscription for Mineralogical Cabinet,	1,603.34	
" John C. Gray's Donation for Mathematical Prizes, ...	500.00	
		2,423.34
Library.		
For Salaries, Repairs, Binding, &c., as per Table III.,	6,977.60	
From Thomas Hollis's Fund for Books, . .	21.99	
" S. Shapleigh's Legacy "	93.83	
" H. A. Haven's " "	11.18	
" S. Salisbury's Donation, "	61.78	
" Wm. Gray's " "	8,447.70	
" T. W. Ward's Legacy "	96.59	
" U. A. Boyden's Donation "	11.25	
		15,721.92
Professorship of Natural History, for Labor, Repairs, &c., Botanic Garden, ...		1,428.94
Theological Institution,		
For Salaries, Repairs, Fuel, &c., . . .	6,784.38	
" Clapp, Pomeroy, and Andrews Donations,	94.37	
		6,878.75
Law School, for Salaries, Prizes, Current Expenses, &c., per Table IV.		13,221.60
Lawrence Scientific School.		
For Expenses of Professorship of Chemistry, .	3,496.28	
" Count Rumford's Legacy, for Salary of Professor Horsford, ...	2,000.00	
Amounts carried forward, .	$5,496.28	$97,315.88

Amount brought forward, . . .		$ 105,134.21
Fuel. — Amount charged Students in Term Bills, .	$ 6,648.72	
Text-Books. — Amount charged Students in Term Bills,	5,065.78	
Gas. — Amount charged Students in Term Bills,	944.58	
		12,659.08

Library. — Amount charged in Term Bills, to Undergraduates, Resident Graduates, Divinity and Law Students, . . . 3,937.50

Theological Institution. — Amount charged Students for Instruction and Rent of Rooms, ... 2,952.25 ,

Law School.

Amount charged Students for Instruction, .	14,432.77	
Income of Investment in Brattle House, as per Table IV., ...	2,010.37	
		16,443.14

Lawrence Scientific School,

Amount charged Students for Instruction and Supplies in Professor Horsford's Department,	1,700.16	
Amount charged Students for Apparatus in do.,	1,234.40	
" " " Instruction in Professor Eustis's Department, . . .	2,630.00	
Amount charged Students for Instruction in Professor Wyman's Department, . . .	1,135.00	
Received allowance on Abbott Lawrence's Donation, appropriated to pay Professor Agassiz's Salary, ...	1,066.67	
Rec'd from A. & A. Lawrence & Co., Interest,	1,500.00	
" " Ward's Island, . . .	50.00	
		9,316.23

Professorship of Natural History, Amount received for Rent of Garden House, ... 158.10

Leonard Jarvis's Devise, ... 687.31

RECEIPTS EXCLUSIVE OF INCOME.

Subscription for Mineralogical Cabinet, . . .	800.00	
Scholarship of the Class of 1835, . . .	150.00	
George P. Bond (Observer), ...	333.24	
Treasurer received for Mortgages paid off, . .	203,582.67	
		204,865.91
Library, received Wm. Gray's Donation (semiannual),	5,000.00	
" " Subscription for purchase of Books,	1,400.00	
" " Mary Osgood's Legacy, . . .	6,000.00	
		12,400.00

Jackson Medical Fund received on account of a Subscription for the Medical College, ... 5,000.00

Abbott Lawrence's Donation, ... 50,000.00

Professor Horsford, for received from him, ... 200.00

Balances, Sept. 1859 : —

In City Bank, ...	2,418.33	
" hands of Wm. G. Stearns, Steward, . .	13,113.36	
" " Baring Brothers & Co., . .	1,176.16	
		16,707.85

$ 440,461.58

(Continued.)

Amounts brought forward,	$ 5,496.28	$ 97,315.88

For Salary of Professor Eustis, and Current Expenses of Prof. of Engineering, as per Table IV. 2,292.79
For Prof. Eustis, from earnings of his Department, ... 1,500.00
" Salary of Professor Agassiz, . . . 2,250.00
" Professor J. Wyman, for Instruction, . 1,135.00
                    12,674.07

Observatory.
From Edward B. Phillips's Legacy, for Salaries of Director and Assistant Observer, and for Books and Instruments, ... 5,000.00
Geo. P. Bond, for Instruments, Expenses, &c., 463.78
                 5,463.78

Hersey Professorship of Theory and Practice of Physic, for Salary of Dr. Shattuck, ... 333.33
W. N. Boylston's Donation for Medical Prizes, . . . 180.00
Warren Fund for Anatomical Museum, for Insurance and Current Expenses, ... 339.12
Gore Annuitants, Amount paid to them, ... 1,500.00
Daniel Williams's Legacy, paid for Minister and Teacher of Herring Pond and Marshpee Indians, ... 633.33
Sarah Winslow's Donation paid for Minister and Schoolmaster of Tyngsborough, and Commissions, ... 227.92
General Expenses, less by $ 5.70 for Sarah Winslow's Donation, and amount received for Diplomas, ... 10,665.79
Expenses of College Buildings, including Repairs, Gas Fixtures, Fuel and Gas for Lecture-Rooms and Chapel, Superintendent's Salary, care of Rooms and of College Grounds, &c., deducting Special Repairs charged to Individuals, and for Grass sold, 7,222.92
Houses and Lands.
For Alterations, Repairs, &c. . . . . $ 34,283.70
" Taxes for 1858, ... 1,145.93
                 35,429.63

APPROPRIATION OF CAPITAL.

INVESTMENTS AND PAYMENTS OF LIABILITIES.

Treasurer, Investments in Notes and Mortgages, $ 168,618.75
Law School, Investment in Brattle House, . . 2,010.87
Expenditure of Income for Zoölogical Museum, . . 1,912.74
   "   "   Coll. of Engravings, . 400.00
Appleton Chapel Income Account, ... 1,261.77
Gymnasium   "   " 1,547.92
Geo. C. Shattuck, Bequest for Prof. of Anatomy, . 1,070.00
Thomas Lee's Donation, ... 1,078.00
Gymnasium Building, ... 46.16
Contract for Building on " Webb Estate," on acc. ' 21,000.00
Pacific Mills Manufacturing Stock, . . . 49,500.00
                 248,445.71

Balances Sept. 1, 1860 : —
In City Bank, ... 3,783.51
" hands of Wm. G. Stearns, Steward, . . 13,272.25
"   "   Baring Brothers & Co., . . 2,974.34
                 20,030.10

                 $ 440,461.58

ACADEMIC

General

Expenses.

Salaries for the Year, viz. : —

President Walker,	$ 1,250.00	
President Felton,	1,500.00	
Professor Felton,	2,300.00	
" Peirce,	2,300.00	
" Gray,	1,900.00	
" Bowen,	2,300.00	
" Lovering,	2,300.00	
" Torrey,	2,300.00	
" Wyman,	800.00	
" Sophocles,	1,200.00	
" Lowell,	2,300.00	
" Huntington,	2,500.00	
" Child,	2,300.00	
" Lane,	2,300.00	
" Cooke,	2,300.00	
" Eliot, $ 1,200 ; Grant, $ 300,	1,500.00	
Tutors. Jennison,	800.00	
Goodwin,	800.00	
Gurney,	800.00	
Pearce,	722.50	
Abbot,	800.00	
Instructors. Lincoln,	722.50	
Schmitt,	640.00	
Miel, *part of year*,	500.00	
Homer,	500.00	
Proctors. Huntington,	100.00	
Peirce,	100.00	
Bartlett,	100.00	
Warren,	100.00	
Regent, Mr. Lovering,	500.00	
Registrar, " Jennison,	200.00	
Treasurer, " Lawrence,	1,500.00	
Steward, " Stearns,	1,400.00	
Sec. of Overseers, Dr. Shurtleff,	60.00	
		$41,695.00
Rent of President's House, paid to President Walker,	600.00	
For keeping Treasurer's Books and copying Records of the Corporation, paid to Mr. Barbour,	1,000.00	
Grant to Observatory for Current Expenses,	200.00	
		1,800.00
Paid to Account of		
Expenses, General,	$ 8,129.31	
President's Department,	35.09	
Treasurer's "	280.59	
Steward's "	163.39	
Professor Lovering's Department,	200.00	
Amounts carried forward,	$ 8,808.38	$ 43,495.00

No. II.

DEPARTMENT.

Statement.

Income.

Interest on Notes on Mortgages, ...	$ 37,480.80
" from Baring Brothers & Co., and gain on Exchange, ...	44.82
" on Philadelphia and Reading Railroad Bonds,	120.00
" " Law School Investment in Brattle House,	772.92
" " Advance to Professorship of Chemistry, .	64.15
" " " Professor Horsford, . .	21.62
Dividends on Stocks, ...	13,724.00
Annuities, ...	171.31
Rents of Houses and Lands in Cambridge, *net*, .	683.71
" Webb Estate, ...	3,800.00
" President's House, ...	600.00
Term Bills, ...	30,742.50
	$ 88,225.83

Less by Income credited to the following Accounts, viz. : —

In the Academic Department.

Beneficiary Fund to Undergraduates, . .	$ 1,018.25
" " Senior Undergraduates,	60.00
John Glover's Annuity, ...	16.67
Wm. Pennoyer's "	154.64
Abbot Scholarship, ...	100.25
Class of 1814 Scholarship, . . .	115.94
Kirkland "	167.75
Class of 1817 "	70.92
" 1835 "	72.40
Saltonstall "	188.10
Alford --	27.25
Shattuck "	940.00
Walcott "	125.10
James Bowdoin's Legacy, for Prizes (Dissertations),	294.07
W. N. Boylston's Prizes (Elocution), .	136.15
Paul Dudley's Legacy for Dudleian Lectures,	24.50
Hollis Professorship of Divinity (accumulating),	415.30
Professorship of Natural History, . . .	638.21
Thomas Hollis's Legacy, for Library, .	125.40
Samuel Shapleigh's " " " . .	246.85
Horace A. Haven's " " " .	109.70
Thomas W. Ward's " " " . .	253.55
Stephen Salisbury's Donation " .	244.17
Uriah A. Boyden's Donation, . . .	2.45

In the Theological School.

Theological Fund, ...	1,182.92
Jackson Foundation and Fund, . .	883.80
Clapp, Pomeroy, and Andrews Donations, .	191.52
Parkman Professorship, ...	762.66
Hancock "	786.12
Dexter Lectureship, ...	465.73
Amounts carried forward, . .	$ 9,820.37 $ 88,225.83

Amounts brought forward, . . .	$ 8,808.38	$ 43,495.00
Professor Cooke's Department, 2 years, .	400.00	
Committees of Examination, . . .	655.38	
Overseers, ...	322.03	
Services of Undergraduates, . . .	480.00	
College buildings, balance of account, .	7,222.92	
Library, in addition to amount charged to Students, ...	3,040.10	
		20,928.81

$ 64,423.81

PARTICULAR

Dr. *Exhibitions.*

For Amount of " Exhibition " money appropriated and paid to		
Seniors, ...	$ 345.00	
Juniors, ...	155.00	
Sophomores, ...	240.00	
Freshmen, ...	245.00	
		$ 985.00
Balance due this Account, August 31, 1860, . . .	20,683.37
		$ 21,668.37

(Continued.)

Amounts brought forward, . .	$ 9,820.37	$ 88,225.83
Henry Lienow's Legacy, ...	437.36	
Nancy Kendall's "	100.00	
Abraham W. Fuller's Legacy	50.00	
Lewis Gould's "	43.40	
John Foster's "	151.02	

In the Law School.

Isaac Royall's Legacy, ...	397.18
Nathan Dane's Donation, ...	750.00

In the Lawrence Scientific School.

Count Rumford's Legacy, ...	1,906.40
Professorship of Engineering, ...	
T. Lee's Donation for Prof. Wyman's Salary, .	1,078.00

In the Medical School.

Hersey Professorship of Theory and Practice of Physic, ...	333.33
W. N. Boylston's Donation for Medical Prizes,	149.00
" " Books, . .	27.50
Dr. Geo. C. Shattuck's Donation for Dr. Jackson's Salary, ...	1,070.00
Warren Fund for Anatomical Museum, . .	272.00

In the Department of the Observatory.

Sears Fund, ...	449.50
Edward B. Phillips's Legacy, ...	5,000.00

Miscellaneous.

Daniel Williams's Legacy, ...	650.00
Sarah Winslow's Donation, ...	227.92
Christopher Gore's Legacy (Annuity Fund), .	1,500.00
Peter C. Brooks's Donation, ...	955.25
Jackson Medical Fund, ...	404.34
Abbott Lawrence's Bequest, ...	1,524.74

	27,297.31
Leaving Amount of Income during the year, applicable to Salaries and other purposes of the College, ...	$ 60,928.52
Amount of Expenses over Income, . . .	3,495.29
	$ 64,423.81

ACCOUNTS.

Exhibitions.   Cr.

By Balance due this Account August 31, 1859, . . .		$ 20,523.45
One year's Income from Senior Exhibitions, .	$ 60.00	
" " " John Glover's Annuity, .	16.67	
Ward's Island, ...	50.00	
		126.67
Interest to August 1, 1860, ...		1,018.25
		$ 21,668.37

Dr. *Seniors'*

For Exhibitions,	$ 60.00
Balance to new Account,	1,200.00
	$ 1,260.00

Dr. *Saltonstall*

Bequests of Dorothy Saltonstall, Mary

For paid Beneficiaries, Income,	$ 180.00
Balance, August 31, 1860,	3,785.40
	$ 3,965.40

Dr. *Pennoyer*

Annuity of

For paid Beneficiaries, 1859,	$ 150.00
Balance, August 31, 1860,	5,021.28
	$ 5,171.28

Dr. *Alford*

Bequest of

For paid Beneficiary,	$ 25.00
Balance, August 31, 1860,	547.21
	$ 572.21

Dr. *Abbot*

For paid Beneficiary,	$ 100.00
Balance due this Account,	
August 31, 1860, { Principal,	1,635.00
Income,	394.57
	$ 2,129.57

(Continued.)

Exhibitions. Cr.

By Balance August 31, 1859, ...	$ 1,200.00
Interest to August 31, 1860, ...	60.00
	$ 1,260.00

Scholarships. Cr.

Saltonstall, and Leverett Saltonstall.

By Balance this Account,

August 31, 1859, { Principal, . . $ 3,330.00

{ Increase, . . 447.30

$ 3,777.30

Interest to August 31, 1860, ... 188.10

$ 3,965.40

Scholarships. Cr.

W. Pennoyer.

By Balance, August 31, 1859, { Annuity, . . $ 4,444.44

{ Increase, . . 572.20

$ 5,016.64

Annuity received this year, ... 154.64

$ 5,171.28

Scholarship. Cr.

Joanna Alford.

By Balance, August 31, 1859, ...	$ 544.96
Interest to August 31, 1860, ...	27.25
	$ 572.21

Scholarship. Cr.

By Balance August 31, 1859, { Principal, . . $ 1,635.00

{ Income, . . 394.32

$ 2,029.32

Interest to August 31, 1860, ... 100.25

$ 2,129.57

Dr.   *Scholarship of the Class*

For paid Beneficiaries one year's Income, ... $ 114.00
Balance to new Account, August 31, 1860, ... 2,348.65

$ 2,462.65

Dr.   *Kirkland Scholarship*

For Balance to new Account,
August 31, 1860, { Principal, . . $ 2,303.46
Income, . . . 1,219.23
$ 3,522.69

$ 3,522.69

Dr.   *Scholarship of the Class*

For Balance to new Accouut,
August 31, 1860, { Principal, . $ 1,015.00
Income, . . 474.39
$ 1,489.39

$ 1,489.39

Dr.   *Scholarship of the Class*

For Balance to new Account,
August 31, 1860, { Principal, . $ 1,165.00
Income, . 490.47
$ 1,655.47

$ 1,655.47

Dr.   *George C. Shattuck's*

For paid Income to Beneficiaries, ... $ 600.00
Balance, August 31, 1860, ... 11,186.00

$ 11,786.00

(Continued.)

of 1814.   Cr.

By Amount received of Members of the Class, . . .		$ 2,300.00
Income, ...		46.71
Interest to August 31, 1860, ...		115.94
		$ 2,462.65

of the Class of 1815.   Cr.

By Balance, August 31, 1859, { Principal, .	$ 2,303.46		
{ Income, . .	1,051.48		
		$ 3,354.94	
Interest to August 31, 1860, ...		167.75	
		$ 3,522.69	

of 1817.   Cr.

By Balance, August 31, 1859, { Principal, ...		$ 1,015.00
{ Income, . . .		403.47
Interest to August 31, 1860, ...		70.92
		$ 1,489.39

of 1835.   Cr.

By Amount received, ...		$ 1,583.07
Interest to August 31, 1860, ...		72.40
		$ 1,655.47

Bequest, for Scholarships.   Cr.

By Balance, August 31, 1859, { Principal, .	$ 10,000.00		
{ Income, . .	846.00		
		$ 10,846.00	
Dividend on Cocheco Stock, ...		940.00	
		$ 11,786.00	

No. II.

Dr.   *Walcott Fund*

For Balance August 31, 1860, ... $ 2,627.03

$ 2,627.03

Dr.   *Edward Hopkins's*

For paid Books for " Deturs,"   .   .   .   .   .   . $ 133.25
      Balance to new Account, August 31, 1860,   .   .   .   148.60

$ 281.85

Dr.   *James Bowdoin's*

For paid Prizes, ... $ 260.00
      Balance, August 31, 1860, { Principal,   . $ 2,500.00
                           { Income,   .   .   3,456.82
                                            $ 5,956.82

$ 6,216.82

Dr.   *Ward N. Boylston's*

For paid Prizes, ... $ 60.00
      Balance, August 31, 1860, { Principal,   . $ 2,000.00
                           { Income,   .   .   799.16
                                            $ 2,799.16

$ 2,859.16

Dr.   *John C. Gray's Donations*

Two Donations of $ 500 each,
To Balance, ... $ 1,000.00

$ 1,000.00

(Continued.)

for Scholarships.   Cr.

By Amount received, being two Philadelphia and Reading Rail-
    road Bonds of $1,000.00 each, ... $ 2,000.00
    Interest to August 31, 1860, accumulating, ...   627.03
                                          $ 2,627.03

Donation for "Deturs."   Cr.

By received from Treasurer of Hopkins Donation, . . . $ 130.00
    Balance, August 31, 1859, ...   151.85
                                          $ 281.85

Legacy.   Cr.

By Balance due this Account,
    August 31, 1859, { Principal, . . $ 2,500.00
                      { Income, . . 3,422.75
                                      $ 5,922.75
    Interest to August 31, 1860, ...   294.07
                                          $ 6,216.82

Prizes for Elocution.   Cr.

By Balance, August 31, 1859, { Principal, . . $ 2,000.00
                          { Income, . . 723.01
                                      $ 2,723.01
    Interest to August 31, 1860, ...   136.15
                                          $ 2,859.16

for Mathematical Prizes.   Cr.

for Mathematical Prizes.
By received Donation, No. 1, December, 1858, ... $ 500.00
    "   "   No. 2, August, 1859, ...   500.00
                                          $ 1,000.00

No. II.

Dr.   *Hollis Professorship*

For Balance due this Account,
August 31, 1860, { Principal, . . $ 3,998.90
{ Income, . . 4,722.48
$ 8,721.38

$ 8,721.38

Dr.   *Hersey Professorship of*
Composed of the Donations of Ezekiel Hersey, Sarah Derby,

For paid Dr. Shattuck, ... $ 333.33
Balance of Income paid Professor Wyman for Salary, 494.28
$ 827.61
Balance, August 31, 1860, ... 16,677.13
$ 17,504.74

Dr.   *Professorship of*

For paid hire of laborers and other expenses, . . . $ 1,428.94
Balance due this Account, August 31, 1860, . . . 12,703.75

$ 14,132.69

Dr.   *Joshua Fisher's*

For paid Professor Gray, Salary, ... $ 1,713.86
Balance, August 31, 1860, { Principal, . $ 33,664.75
{ Income, . . 612.38
$ 34,277.13
$ 35,990.99

Dr.   *Jonathan Phillips's*

For paid Salaries and Grants, — Salary of Greek Professor, . $ 600.00
Balance, August 31, 1860, ... 10,000.00

$ 10,600.00

(Continued.)

of Divinity.   Cr.

By Balance due this Account,

August 31, 1859, { Principal, . . $ 3,998.90
                 { Income, . . 4,307.18
                                                            ———————— $ 8,306.08
Interest to August 31, 1860, ... 415.30
                                                                      ————————
                                                                      $ 8,721.38

Anatomy, Surgery, and Physic.   Cr.

Esther Sprague, Abner Hersey, and John Cumming.

By Balance, August 31, 1859, ... $ 16,677.13
    Interest to August 31, 1860, ... 827.61

                                                                      ————————
                                                                      $ 17,504.74

Natural History.   Cr.

By Balance due this Account, August 31, 1859, . . . $ 13,336.38
    Rent on cost of addition to Garden House, . . . 158.10
    Interest to August 31, 1860, ... 638.21
                                                                      ————————
                                                                      $ 14,132.69

Legacy.   Cr.

By Balance due this Account, August 31, 1859, . . . $ 34,277.13
    Interest for one year to August 31, 1860, . . . 1,713.86

                                                                      ————————
                                                                      $ 35,990.99

Donation.   Cr.

By Amount received, ... $ 10,000.00
    Interest on Mortgage, ... 600.00
                                                                      ————————
                                                                      $ 10,600.00

No. II.

Dr. *John McLean's*

For paid Professor Torrey, Salary, ...	$ 2,050.62

Balance, August 31, 1860, { Principal, . $ 25,544.15
                            { Income, . . 15,468.16
                            ——— $ 41,012.31

$ 43,062.93

Dr. *Plummer Foundation for the Support*

For paid on Account of Salary of Plummer Professor, . . $ 1,191.44
Balance, August 31, 1860, ... 23,828.75

$ 25,020.19

No. III.

LIBRARY.

Dr. *General*

For paid Salary to Mr. Sibley, ...	$ 1,400.00
" " " " Room Rent, . . .	60.00
" " " Mr. E. Abbot, Jr., ...	1,300.00
" " " J. W. Harris, ...	400.00
" " Binding, ...	272.01
" " Fuel, ...	323.25
" " Books, ...	349.77
" " A. S. Waitt, Sundries, ...	571.00
" " S. Palmer, Drain, ...	280.08
" " Water Works, ...	113.85
" " Janitor, Stationery, &c., ...	1,907.64

$ 6,977.60

Dr. *Thomas Hollis's*

For paid for Books, ... $ 67.30
Balance, August 31, 1860, ... 2,614.87

$ 2,682.17

(Continued.)

Legacy. Cr.

By Balance due this Account, August 31, 1859, . . . $ 41,012.31
    Interest to August 31, 1860, ... 2,050.62

$43,062.93

of a Professor of the "Philosophy of the Heart," &c. Cr.

By Balance, August 31, 1859, Principal and Income, . . $ 23,828.75
    Interest to August 31, 1860, ... 1,191.44

$ 25,020.19

No. III.

LIBRARY.

Statement. Cr.

By Amount received from Divinity Students, . . $ 82.50
    "   "   " Law   " . . . 802.50
    "   "   " Undergraduates, . . 2,970.00
    "   "   " Resident Graduates, . . 82.50
                                                $ 3,937.50
    Income for Balance, ... 3,040.10

$ 6,977.60

Fund for Library. Cr.

By Balance, August 31, 1859, { Principal, . . $ 2,222.23
                          { Income, . . . 334.54
                                            $ 2,556.77
    Interest to August 31, 1860, ... 125.40

$ 2,682.17

No. III.

Dr.   *Samuel Shapleigh's*

For paid for Books, ... $ 141.77
    Balance, August 31, 1860, ... 5,102.36

                                                  $ 5,244.13

Dr.   *Horace A. Haven's*

For paid for Books, ... $ 11.18
    Balance, August 31, 1860, ... 2,292.82

                                                  $ 2,304.00

Dr.   *Uriah A. Boyden's*

For paid Professor Lovering, ... $ 11.25
    Balance, August 31, 1860, ... 45.06

                                                  $ 56.31

Dr.   *Thomas W. Ward's*

To paid for Books, ... $ 349.70
    Balance, August 31, 1860, ... 5,055.25

                                                  $ 5,404.95

Dr.   *Stephen Salisbury's*

                                  The Income to be expended

To paid for Books, ... $ 734.35
    Balance, ... 4,556.54

                                                  $ 5,290.89

Dr.   *William Gray's Donation*

        The Principal of this Fund, amounting in 5 years to $ 25,000,

To paid for Books, ... $ 5,889.81
    Balance, ... 1,610.19

                                                  $ 7,500.00

(Continued.)

Fund for Library.   Cr.

By Balance, August 31, 1859,	$ 3,777.77	
Income,	1,219.51	
		$ 4,997.28
Interest to August 31, 1860,		246.85
		$ 5,244.13

Legacy.   Cr.

By Balance, August 31, 1859,	$ 2,194.30
Interest to August 31, 1860,	109.70
	$ 2,304.00

Donation.   Cr.

By Balance, August 31' 1859,	$ 53.86
Interest to August 31, 1860,	2.45
	$ 56.31

Legacy for Books.   Cr.

By received Amount of Bequest, April, 1859,	$ 5,000.00
Interest to August 31, 1860,	404.95
	$ 5,404.95

Donation.   Cr.

in the purchase of Books.

By received Donation,	$ 5,000.00
Interest to August 31, 1860,	290.89
	$ 5,290.89

for Library.   Cr.

is to be expended in purchasing Books for the Library.

By Amount received,	$ 7,500.00
	$ 7,500.00

No. III.

Dr.   *Subscription for*

The following sums were subscribed to form a Fund, the Income

To Balance, ... $ 6,067.00

$ 6,067.00

No. IV.

ACCOUNTS OF

THEOLOGICAL

Dr.   *General*

For paid Salary to Professor Francis, ... $ 2,200.00
      "   "   Noyes, ...   2,200.00
    Repairs, Superintendent, &c.   .   .   .   938.38
    Beneficiaries, ...   846.00
    Dr. Hedge's Salary, as Professor of Ecclesiastical History,   300.00
    Dr. Ellis's Salary, as Professor of Systematic Theology,   300.00
    Balance to new Account, August 31, 1860,   .   .   .   26,569.67

$ 33,354.05

(Continued.)

College Library.   Cr.

to be expended in the purchase of Books for the Library.

By Balance August 31, 1859,	. . . . . .	$ 4,667.00
" received of Sidney Bartlett,	. . . .	100.00
" " Graduates,	. . . .	600.00
" " H. S. Higginson,	. . . .	50.00
" " J. J. Higginson,	. . . .	50.00
" " Henry A. Whitney,	. . . . . .	500.00
" " James Savage,	. . . . . .	100.00
		$ 6,067.00

No. **IV.**

PROFESSIONAL SCHOOLS.

SCHOOL.

Statement.   Cr.

By Balance due this Account, August 31, 1859, . . .		$ 25,778.19
Amount of Term Bills, for Instruction, Library, Rent, &c.,		2,852.25
By Income from Consolidated Fund for Hancock Professorship, ...	$ 786.12	
Income from Dexter Lectureship Fund, . .	465.73	
" " Consolidated Fund for Parkman Professorship, ...	762.66	
Income from Jackson Foundation and Fund, .	795.42	
" " Henry Lienow's Legacy, . .	487.36	
" " Nancy Kendall's " . .	100.00	
Abraham W. Fuller's Legacy, ...	50.00	
Lewis Gould's "	43.40	
Received from Society for Promoting Theological Education, salaries, ...	600.00	
		$ 32,171.13
Interest on this Account to August 31, 1860, .	. .	1,182.92
		$ 33,354.05

Dr.   No. IV.

Consolidated Fund

Donations of Sarah Jackson,

For paid Theological School, for Beneficiaries, four and one half
per cent on the fund for one year, ... $ 795.42
.   Balance, August 31, 1860, ...   17,764.85

$ 18,560.27

Dr.   *Clapp, Pomeroy, and*

Donations of Joshua Clapp, William

For paid Theological School, Income, &c., ... $ 94.37
Balance, August 31, 1860, ...   3,984.26

$ 4,078.63

Dr.   *Consolidated Fund for Parkman*

Composed of the Donations of Samuel Parkman and Francis Parkman,

To paid Theological School, ... $ 762.66
Balance, August 31, 1860, ...   15,253.15

$ 16,015.81

Dr.   *Consolidated Fund for Hancock*

Composed of the Legacy of Thomas Hancock, and of the Donations of

To paid Theological School, ... $ 786.12
Balance, August 31, 1860, ...   15,722.31

$ 16,508.43

Dr.   *Dexter Lectureship*

The Legacy of

To paid Theological School, ... $ 465.73
Balance, August 31, 1860, ...   9,314.65

$ 9,780.38

Dr.   *Samuel Hoar's Legacy*

For amount of Legacy, ... $ 1,000.00

(Continued.)

for Theological Students.   Cr.

Thomas Cary, and George Chapman.

By Balance, August 31, 1860, $\begin{cases} \text{Principal,} \\ \text{Income,} \end{cases}$ $ 15,582.69
                                                                    2,093.78
                                                             ——————— $ 17,676.47
          Interest to August 31, 1860, ...   883.80

                                                             $ 18,560.27

Andrews Donations.   Cr.

Pomeroy, and Hannah C. Andrews.

By Balance, August 31, 1859, $\begin{cases} \text{Principal,} \\ \text{Income,} \end{cases}$. $ 3,857.90
                                                                    29.21
                                                             ——————— $ 3,887.11
          Interest to August 31, 1860, ...   191.52

                                                             $ 4,078.63

Professorship of Pulpit Eloquence.   Cr.

and of the Legacies of George Partridge and Eliphalet Porter.

By Balance, August 31, 1859, ... $ 15,253.15
          Interest to August 31, 1860, ...   762.66

                                                             $ 16,015.81

Professorship of Hebrew, &c.   Cr.

the Society for Promoting Theological Education and Samuel Sewall.

By Balance, August 31, 1859, ... $ 15,722.31
          Interest to August 31, 1860, ...   786.12

                                                             $ 16,508.43

on Biblical Literature.   Cr.

Samuel Dexter.

By Balance, August 31, 1859, ... $ 9,314.65
          Interest to August 31, 1860, ...   465.73

                                                             $ 9,780.38

for Theological Institution.   Cr.

By received amount of Legacy, March, 1857, ... $ 1,000.00

No. IV.

Dr.   *Lewis Gould's*

For Income to Theological School, ... $ 43.40
    Balance, August 31, 1860, ... 867.94

                                                     $ 911.34

LAW

Dr.   *General*

For Balance due this Account, August 31, 1859, . . . $ 19,035.66
For paid Insurance, ... $ 1·25.00
    Repairs and other expenses, ... 2,138.39
    Books purchased, ... 1,330.95
    Furniture, Printing, Stationery, &c., . . 1,180.30
                                          4,774.64
    Salary to Professor Parker, ... 2,000.00
      "   "   Parsons, . . . 3,000.00
      "   "   Washburn, . . . 3,000.00
                                          8,000.00
    Assistant Steward, ... 500.00
    Librarian, ... 200.00
                                          700.00
    Prizes to Students for Dissertations, . . . 200.00
    Instruction remitted, ... 225.00
    Loans, ... 200.00
    Investment in Brattle House, ... 1,905.25

                                        $ 35,040.55

Dr.   *Investment of Law School*

To Balance, August 31, 1860, ... $ 30,150.16
    Repairs, Furniture, Gas Fixtures, &c., ... 1,132.33
    Interest on Funds provided by the College, . . . 772.92

                                        $ 32,055.41

LAWRENCE

Dr.   -   *General*

For Balance, August 31, 1859,
    Finishing Laboratory, and for Expenses in Geological Depart-
      ment, ... $ 4,470.39
    Chemicals, &c. in the Laboratory, ... 1,465.63

                                          $ 5,936.02

(Continued.)

Legacy. Cr.

By amount received of Executor, ...	$ 867.94
Interest to August 31, 1860, ...	43.40
	$ 911.34

SCHOOL.

Statement. Cr.

By Rent of Brattle House, to August, 1860 (12 months), . .	$ 2,010.37
Amount of Term Bills, ... $ 15,235.27	
Deduct amount paid Library, . . . 802.50	
	14,432.77
Income of Isaac Royall's Legacy, ... 750.00	
" Nathan Dane's Donation, ... 397.18	
" John Foster's Legacy, ... 151.02	
	1,298.20
Balance to Debit of Law School, ...	17,299.21

$ 35,040.55

Funds in Brattle House. Cr.

By received Rents of Brattle House, ...	$ 2,010.37
Balance, August 31, 1860, ...	30,045.04
	$ 32,055.41

SCIENTIFIC SCHOOL.

Statement. Cr.

Received from Professorship of Engineering, excess of Earnings,	$ 337.21
" " " Chemistry, ...	1,507.34
" " Abbott Lawrence's Bequest, ...	1,841.41
Balance, ...	2,250.06
	$ 5,936.02

No. IV.

Dr.   *Professor*

For Balance of Account, August 31, 1859, ... $ 427.13
   Interest to August 31, 1860, ... 21.62
                                                       $ 448.75

Dr.   *Professorship of*

Paid Expenses in Professor Horsford's Department,
   Services of Janitor and Assistants, . . . $ 526.62
   ' Fuel, ... 178.50
   Current Expenses, including Chemicals, . . 2,191.16
   Assistant Steward, ... 200.00
                                               3,096.28
Interest on this Account to August 31, 1860, ... 64.15
Prof. E. N. Horsford, *Grant*, ... 400.00
Laboratory and Geological Department, ... 1,507.34
                                           $ 5,067.77

Dr.   *Count Rumford's*

For paid Professor Horsford's Salary, ... $ 2,000.00
       Professorship of Chemistry, excess of Income, . . . 483.92
   Balance, August 31, 1860, ... 44,888.50
                                         $ 47,372.42

Dr.   *Professorship of*

For paid Current Expenses, ... $ 292.79
   " Assistants, ... 400.00
   " Assistant Steward, ... 100.00
                                     $ 792.79
" " Professor Eustis's stated Salary, . . $ 1,500.00
" " " " additional Salary,
   from income of this Department, $ 750.00
" Amount to Account of Professor Eustis
   for do., ... 750.00
                            1,500.00
                                     3,000.00
Amount to Credit of Lawrence Scientific School, . . . 337.21
   Balance, August 31, 1860, ... 25,000.00
                                        $ 29,130.00

(Continued.)

Horsford.   Cr.

By received of Professor Horsford, ...	$ 200.00
Balance, August 31, 1860, ...	248.75
	$ 448.75

Chemistry.   Cr.

By Balance, August 31, 1859, ...	$ 756.70
Amount received for Instruction and Supplies, and Apparatus, in Professor Horsford's Department, ...	2,934.56
By received from Rumford Legacy, ...	483.92
Balance, August 31, 1860, ...	892.59
	$ 5,067.77

Legacy.   Cr.

By received of Count Rumford's Trustees, Paris, ...	$ 577.52
In hands " " "	6,000.00
By Balance due this Account, August 31, 1859, . . .	38,888.50
Interest to August 31, 1860, ...	1,906.40
	$ 47,372.42

Engineering.   Cr.

By Balance, August 31, 1859, ...	$ 25,000.00
Interest for one year, to August 31, 1860, from A. & A. Lawrence & Co., ...	1,500.00
Amount of Term Bills for Instruction, ...	2,630.00
	$ 29,130.00

No. IV.

Dr.   *Abbott Lawrence's*

Bequest for the

To paid Professor Agassiz's salary, ... $ 2,250.00
    Laboratory and Geological Department, ... 1,841.41
    Balance, August 31, 1860, ... 50,000.00

                                                             $ 54,091.41

MEDICAL

Dr.   *Ward N. Boylston's Donation*

For paid Prizes, ... $ 180.00
    Balance, August 31, 1860, ... 2,949.52

                                                             $ 3,129.52

Dr.   *Ward N. Boylston's*

For Balance, August 31, 1860, ... $ 577.50

                                                             $ 577.50

Dr.   *George C. Shattuck's Donation for*

For paid Dr. J. B. S. Jackson, Income, ... $ 1,070.00
    Balance, August 31, 1860, ... 14,000.00

                                                      $ 15,070.00

Dr.   *J. C. Warren's Fund*

For paid Expenses and Insurance on Museum, ... $ 339.12
Balance, August 31, 1860, { Principal, . . $ 5,000.00
                                { Income, . . . 504.44

                                                    5,504.44

                                                       $ 5,843.56

Dr.   *Jackson*

A Fund given for the benefit

To Balance, ... $ 10,404.34

                                                      $ 10,404.34

(Continued.)

Bequest. Cr.

Scientific School.

By received Donation and Interest, ...	$ 52,566.67
Interest to August 31, 1860, ...	1,524.74
	$ 54,091.41

SCHOOL.

for Medical Prizes. Cr.

By Balance, August 31, 1859, ...	$ 2,980.52
Interest for one year, ...	149.00
	$ 3,129.52

Donation for Books. Cr.

By Balance, August 31, 1859, ...	$ 550.00
Interest for one year, ...	27.50
	$ 577.50

Professor of Anatomy in Medical School. Cr.

By amount received, ...	$ 14,000.00
Received Dividend on Atlantic Mills, ...	440.00
" " Stark Mills, ...	630.00
	$ 15,070.00

for Anatomical Museum. Cr.

By Balance, August 31, 1859, { Principal, . .	$ 5,000.00	
Income, . .	571.56	
		$ 5,571.56
Interest to August 31, 1860, ...		272.00
		$ 5,843.56

Medical Fund. Cr.

of the Medical School.

By amount received, ...	$ 10,000.00
Interest to August 31, 1860, . . .	404.34
	$ 10,404.34

ASTRONOMICAL

Dr. *Sears*

Balance to new Capital, August 31, 1860, ... $ 9,439.46

$ 9,439.46

Dr. *Edward B. Phillips's*

For paid Salary of Mr. G. P. Bond, . . .	$ 2,200.00	
" " Assistants, ...	1,839.00	
		$ 4,039.00
" " for Books and Printing, . .	94.26	
" " " Instruments and Appara	866.74	
		961.00
Balance, August 31, 1860, ...		100,000.00
		$ 105,000.00

Dr. *Quincy Fund*

Balance of 1860 Account, ⌐. . . . . $ 1,235.14

MISCEL-

FUNDS APPROPRIATED

Dr. *Peter C. Brooks's*

For Balance, August 31, 1860, { Principal, ... $ 10,000.00
{ Income, . . . 10,060.83

$ 20,060.83

No. V.

OBSERVATORY.

Fund. (*Accumulating.*)   Cr.

By Balance, August 31, 1859, Capital, ... $ 8,989.96
         Interest to August 31, 1860, 5 per cent, . . .   449.50

                                            $ 9,439.46

Legacy for Salaries, Instruments, &c.   Cr.

By Balance, August 31, 1859, ... $ 100,000.00
         Interest to August 31, 1860, ...   5,000.00

                                            $ 105,000.00

for Observatory.   Cr.

By Amount due to balance Account, ... $ 1,235.14

No. VI.

LANEOUS.

TO SPECIAL PURPOSES.

Donation for building House for the President.   Cr.

By Balance, August 31, 1859, { Principal, . . $ 10,000.00
                            { Income, . .   9,105.58
                                         19,105.58
        Interest to August 31, 1860, ...   955.25

                                            $ 20,060.83

No. VI.

Dr. *Appleton Chapel*

To paid for Singing and Music,		$ 493.93
" Sexton,		135.00
" Fuel,		105.00
" Sweeping, &c.,		84.92
" extra expense of Organ,		266.00
" for Reading-Desk,		176.92
		$ 1,261.77

Dr. *John Foster's Legacy. Income appropriated*

For Income this year to Law School,	$ 151.02
Balance, August 31, 1860,	3,020.48
	$ 3,171.50

Dr. *Gray Fund for*
Income for sustaining the "Gray

To paid Mr. Thies,	$ 400.00
Balance,	15,692.27
	$ 16,092.27

Dr. *Devise of Leonard*
Devised without

To Balance,	$ 12,487.31
	$ 12,487.31

Dr. *Gymnasium*
Donation of " a Graduate "

To paid for Building, &c.,	$ 9,534.21
	$ 9,534.21

Dr. *Gymnasium*

To paid A. M. Hewlett, Salary	$ 750.00
" A. S. Waitt, alterations, &c.,	270.22
" Labor, Gas, Fuel, &c.,	527.70
Balance,	342.08
	$ 1,890.00

(Continued.)

(*Income Account.*) Cr.

By Balance, August 31, 1859,	$ 331.68
Received Pew Rents,	864.00
Balance, August 31, 1860,	66.09
	$ 1,261.77

alternately to Theological, Law, and Medical Schools. Cr.

By Balance, August 31, 1859, $\begin{cases} \text{Principal,} & \$ 2,000.00 \\ \text{Income,} & 1,020.48 \end{cases}$

	$ 3,020.48
Interest to August 31, 1860,	151.02
	$ 3,171.50

Collection of Engravings. Cr.
Collection of Engravings."

By received of William Gray, Principal and Income,	$ 15,444.35
Income, &c.,	647.92
	$ 16,092.27

Jarvis, of Baltimore. Cr.
restrictions.

By received Real Estate,	$ 11,800.00
" " Income,	687.31
	$ 12,487.31

Building. Cr.
for Building a Gymnasium.

By received, December, 1858,	$ 8,000.00
Balance,	1,534.21
	$ 9,584.21

(*Income Account.*) Cr.

By received from students,	$ 1,890.00
	$ 1,890.00

No. VI.

Dr.   *Mary Osgood's*
                        Income after a certain time to be appropriated
To Balance, ... $ 6,000.00

FUNDS IN TRUST FOR PURPOSES

Dr.   *Daniel Williams's Legacy for Preaching*
For paid C. Marston, for Herring Pond Indians, .   . $ 200.00
  Paid Charles Marston, Treasurer of the Marsh-
    pee Indians, two thirds of same,   .   .   . 433.33
                                                           ————————
                                                                       $ 633.33
  Balance, August 31, 1860, { Principal,   .   . 13,000.00
                            { Income,   .   . 2,256.70
                                                   ————————
                                                               15,256.70
                                                           ————————
                                                                       $ 15,890.03

Dr.   *Sarah Winslow's*
For paid Rev. N. O. Chaffin, Minister of Tyngsborough,
    half the net income of this Fund, to January 1,
    1860, ... $ 111.11
  Paid P. Allen, for services as Schoolmaster in Tyngs-
    borough, half the net income of this Fund,   111.11
                                                   ————————
                                                               $ 222.22
  ·Two and a half per cent commission on Income, carried to
    account of Expenses, ...   5.70
  Balance, August 31, 1860, ...   4,558.34
                                                           ————————
                                                                       · $ 4,786.26

Dr.   *Gray Fund for*
                            Income for sustaining a Museum
To paid Professor Agassiz, ... $ 1,912.74
  Balance, ... 51,500.00
                                                           ————————
                                                                       $ 53,412.74

No. VII.

Dr.   STOCK

To Income account, more paid than received during the year, . $ 3,495.29
  Manufacturing Stocks, made par, ... 870.00
  Boylston Museum Account,   .   · 10,790.72
  Balance, August 31, 1860, ... 172,604.25
                                                           ————————
                                                                       $ 187,760.26

(Continued.)

Legacy.   Cr.

for the purchase of Books.

By received, ... $ 6,000.00

NOT CONNECTED WITH THE COLLEGE.

the Gospel among the Indians.   Cr.

By Balance, August 31, 1859, { Principal, . . $ 13,000.00
{ Income, . . 2,240.03

         —————— $ 15,240.03

Interest for the year 1860, ... 650.00

         $ 15,890.03

Donation.   Cr.

By Balance, August 31, 1859, ... $ 4,558.34
Interest for the year 1860, ... 227.92

         $ 4,786.26

Zoölogical Museum.   Cr.

of Comparative Zoölogy.

By received of William Gray, January, 1859, and Income, . $ 50,412.74
Income, ... 3,000.00

         $ 53,412.74

No. VII.

ACCOUNT.   Cr.

By Balance, ... $ 187,760.26

         $ 187,760.26

No. VIII.

The following Account exhibits the State of the Property, as embraced and balanced in the Treasurer's Books, August 31, 1860. (The College Buildings, with the Library, and other Property contained in them belonging to the College, and the Grounds under and adjoining the same, have no pecuniary value attached to them in the Treasurer's Books.)

Notes and Mortgages,				$ 541,723.60
Jonathan Phillips's Donation Invested in Mortgage,			$ 10,000.00	
New York Central Railroad Bonds, valued at			10,000.00	
Philadelphia and Reading " " " "			2,000.00	
City of Albany Stock,			6,000.00	
In hands of Count Rumford's Trustees in Paris,			10,000.00	
				38,000.00
Bank Stock.	Boston,	294 shares,	14,457.75	
	Merchants',	50 "	5,000.00	
	Fitchburg,	24 "	2,403.00	
	New England,	30 "	3,000.00	
	Charles River,	60 "	6,000.00	
	Massachusetts,	12 "	3,000.00	
				33.860.75
Manufacturing Stock.				
	Merrimack,	17 shares,	17,000.00	
	Boston,	10 "	7,000.00	
	Stark,	17 "	17,000.00	
	Atlantic,	15 "	11,980.00	
	Cocheco,	20 "	10,000.00	
	Great Falls,	11 "	2,050.00	
	Amoskeag,	12 "	12,000.00	
	Appleton,	5 "	5,000.00	
	Hamilton,	5 "	5,000.00	
	Massachusetts,	5 "	5,000.00	
	Suffolk,	5 "	5,000.00	
	Manchester,	3 "	3,000.00	
	Pacific,	55 "	49,500.00	
				149,530.00
Railroad Stock.	Western, 50 shares,		5,000.00	
	Pittsfield and North Adams, 50 shares,		5,000.00	
				10,000.00
Annuities.	William Pennoyer's		4,444.44	
	John Glover's		350.00	
				4,794.44
Real Estate.	(Houses and Lands,)		139,415.30	
	Pews in First Parish Church, Cambridge,		410.00	
	Ward's Island, in Boston Harbor,		1,200.00	
	Reversion of Buildings on Brattle Street, Boston,		1,000.00	
	Webb Estate, Boston,		28,237.58	
	Jarvis Estate, Baltimore,		11,800.00	
	Brattle House, Cambridge, being the Investment of Law School Funds,		30,045.04	
				212,107.92
Amount carried forward,				$ 990,016.71

No. VIII.

And the foregoing Property represents the following Funds and Balances, and is answerable for the same.

Funds appropriated to the Academic Department

Balance of Stock Account,	$172,604.25
Exhibitions,	20,683.37
Exhibitions (Senior),	1,200.00
	$194,487.62

Scholarships.

Saltonstall,	3,785.40
Pennoyer,	5,021.28
Alford,	547.21
Abbot,	2,029.57
Class of 1814,	2,848.65
" " 1815 (Kirkland),	1,655.47
" " 1817,	1,489.39
" " 1835,	8,522.69
Shattuck,	11,186.00
Walcott,	2,627.03
	34,212.69

Edward Hopkins's Donation for " Deturs,"	148.60
James Bowdoin's Legacy,	5,956.82
Boylston Fund, Prizes for Elocution,	2,799.16
Paul Dudley's Legacy,	514.49
Hollis Professorship of Divinity,	8,721.38
" " of Mathematics,	3,568.89
Alford Professorship,	26,427.28
Boylston "	26,988.00
Hersey "	16,677.13
Erving "	3,333.34
Professorship of Natural History,	12,703.75
Fisher Professorship,	84,277.13
Eliot "	20,590.00
Jonathan Phillips's Donation,	10,000.00
Smith Professorship,	22,037.93
McLean "	41,012.31
Perkins "	20,000.00
Plummer "	23,828.75
Fund for Permanent Tutors,	20,978.13
Leonard Jarvis's Devise and Income,	12,487.31
	313,050.40

Library Funds.

Thomas Hollis's Bequest,	2,614.87
Samuel Shapleigh's "	5,102.36
Horace A. Haven's "	2,292.82
Uriah A. Boyden's Donation,	45.06
Thomas W. Ward's Bequest,	5,055.25
Stephen Salisbury's Donation,	4,556.54
Subscription for Library,	6,067.00
	25,733.90

Amount carried forward,	$567,484.61

Lightning Source UK Ltd.
Milton Keynes UK
UKHW010642170119
335572UK00014B/1775/P